Happiness

Happiness

FINDERS, KEEPERS

MARY ELLEN EDMUNDS

МⓇ
DESERET
BOOK
SALT LAKE CITY, UTAH

First printing in hardbound 1999
First printing in paperbound 2003

Visit us at deseretbook.com

Library of Congress Cataloging-in-Publication Data

Edmunds, Mary Ellen, 1940–
    Happiness, finders, keepers / Mary Ellen Edmunds.
        p.   cm.
    ISBN 1-57345-556-3 (hardbound)
    ISBN 1-59038-265-X (paperbound)
        1. Happiness—Religious aspects—Church of Jesus Christ of Latter-day
    Saints.   2. Christian life—Mormon authors.   I. Title.
    BX8643.H35E35   1999
    248.4—dc21   99-15730
                                                                                  CIP

Printed in the United States of America   72076-029P
Publishers Printing, Salt Lake City, UT

10   9   8   7   6   5   4   3   2   1

For my family:
I'm surrounded by happiness!

CONTENTS

Preface   ix

1 Happification   1

2 The Great Plan of Happiness   7

3 Some Ways to Find, Keep,
   and Share Happiness   23

4   A Little Bit of Stress Goes a Long, Long Way   47

5 Adversity and Afflictions   77

6 Wendell's Triumph over Adversity   95

7 Gratitude: The Happy Attitude!   109

8 Humor and a Happy Heart   134

9 A Merry Heart Doeth Good like a Medicine   148

10 O Remember, Remember   168

11 Remembering PK and Lewie   189

12 Happily Ever After   202

   Index   209

PREFACE

WHY WOULD I SET OUT to write a book about happiness? Doesn't everyone already know what it feels like and how to find it? Perhaps not. It occurs to me that happiness—like health—is one of the things most sought after yet often most elusive in life. It can't be purchased, it can't be forced, and it can't be "stored." But it can be renewed day by day and even hour by hour.

I've had people tell me that speaking and writing of happiness at a time when the world is filled with so much contention, sorrow, inequity, and evil feels like an "oxymoron"—it doesn't make sense. To me there was never a time when we had a greater need for happiness and for the peace, contentment, serenity, hope, gratitude, and joy that are part of it.

I am convinced that even with the heavy burdens, the awful injustices, and the tragedies in the world, there is happiness all around us. We must be the finders and the keepers—those who are aware of and who cherish this holy, abundant blessing.

I know there are stories I have shared in this book that would be more detailed or interesting if others had written them. My brother John might have written better the chapter about our dear father's experience with his friend Lewie. My mother or some other family member could have shared their perspective of Mom's stroke. Susan, Wendy Sue, or "Grandma J" might have done greater justice to the chapter about their dear Wendell. I apologize if I've not done as complete or beautiful a job as they'd have done.

I thank those whose happy examples have lifted me so high and shown me such clear and interesting paths to happiness. Thank you, happy people, for your influence in my life (especially my parents and brothers and sisters). It helps so much to have a cheerful light to show the rest of us the way.

When I look back at the experience of writing this book about happiness, I will remember Carolyn and her peaceful home at the beach, and the privilege I had to be in that setting for some of the early work and then for the final writing of many of the chapters. What a blessing! Can you dedicate a book to a home?

I'm grateful to my friends at Deseret Book, especially Emily Watts, my editor, for encouragement and significant help in this challenging, wonderful project of writing a book.

A portion of the proceeds from this book will be donated to temple funds that will help some to attend and receive the happiness and peace they've been waiting for for such a long, long time (or even for a short time).

I hope you will enjoy your reading experience, and that in addition to finding and keeping this gift of happiness, you'll freely and generously pass the happiness along.

Chapter 1

HAPPIFICATION

THIS IS A BOOK ABOUT HAPPINESS—what it is, how it feels, why it matters, and how to find and keep it. It's also a book about ways in which we can share happiness with others—be *happifiers*, living so that our influence on people and situations is *happifying*.

As some of these may be new words to the reader, let me explain. I actually thought I had made up a bunch of new words, but some of them are in the dictionary! And the meaning in the dictionary is just what I had thought it would be. So here we go:

To *happify* is to make happy, as in "Beautiful sunrises and sunsets *happify* me." Isn't that wonderful! *Happifiers* are the people, things, or experiences that lift the spirits and burdens of those who come within their influence, as in "Children are important *happifiers* in my life!" I think Elder Neal A. Maxwell was describing *happifiers* when he said, "Pleasure usually takes the form of 'me' and 'now,' while joy is 'us' and 'always'" (*The Smallest Part* [Salt Lake City: Deseret Book, 1973], p. 23). Happiness and joy come from being *happifiers*.

Happifying (this one's not in the dictionary) is something that adds to the process of *happification* (also not in the dictionary), as in "To be able to go to the temple is a *happifying* experience." When we have the privilege of finding and holding tight to happiness, we might say that we are *happified*, or that we have achieved *happification*. There. Now you know.

It is my hope that those who read this book and begin doing something, however small, differently from the way they've been doing it may feel *happified!*

There are many phrases we use to wish each other this wonderful gift, this blessing of happiness: "Have a happy day!" "Happy birthday!" "Happy Valentine's Day!" "Happy New Year!" "Happy holidays!" "Happy trip!" "Happy trails!" (or should that be "Happy trials"?) "Happy landings!" And there's one that used to be more common than it is now: "Happy Christmas!"

I still have a little greeting card that someone gave me at least thirty years ago; it says: "Happy winter, Happy spring, Happy happy *everything!*"

We use the word to describe feelings and circumstances, such as "I'm as happy as a clam." (I use that expression without having the slightest idea *why* or even *if* a clam is happy! How can anyone tell whether it is or not? Maybe it's that perpetual "shell smile" or something.) "Happy is as happy does." "I'm so happy I could cry!" "What makes *you* so happy?" "If you're happy and you know it, tell your face!" "If it weren't for _____, I sure would be happy." "When _____, I know I'll be happy."

What *is* happiness? Peace? A pleasant surprise? A feeling in the heart? Is happiness always obvious on the outside—on our faces, in our voices, in our actions? Is it only evident when we laugh out loud, clap our hands, or dance or "party"? Are we ever happy when we're weeping? Are we happy when we're being noisy, or when we're very quiet? Either? Both?

Maybe our view of happiness is too narrow or restrictive, and so we don't recognize it when it's with us in our hearts and souls, in our days, and in so much that is all around us.

Why did I choose a title that included "Finders, Keepers"? I can remember the day that title jumped into my head and heart. It seemed so right, the thought that as we're able to *find* happiness, we'll also have figured out how to *keep* it. When it's the real thing, it tends to stay with us. Saying we've found happiness is a way of saying we've worked for it, we've earned it. It also is a way of saying that we've come to recognize it, enjoy it, and cherish it. It is safeguarded and protected deep inside of us.

President David O. McKay said, "Man is the creator of his own happiness. It is the aroma of life lived in harmony with high ideals. For what a man has he may be dependent upon others; what he is rests with him alone" (Conference Report, October 1955, p. 8).

I agree. We do create our own happiness. And we need to learn to keep it once we find it. Elder Jack H. Goaslind expressed it beautifully: "I am convinced if we are to have happiness in our hearts, we must learn how to preserve it, in our hearts, [even] in the midst of trouble and trial" (*Church News*, 13 April 1986, p. 20).

In this book I wish to speak of genuine happiness—the real thing—as much as I can. This is no small task, as there is so much in our world and our culture that masquerades as happiness. There are feelings that try to substitute for the real thing but turn out instead to be fleeting pleasures or transitory tastes of self-gratification. I wish to speak of the deep feelings in the soul, including peace of heart, genuine gratitude, sweet contentment, bright hope, and pure joy.

Elder James E. Talmage has contrasted pleasure and happiness in a profound way, and although I'm almost uncomfortable using such a pleasant word as *pleasure* to mean practically the opposite of *happiness*, I have found his explanation to be very helpful:

> Happiness includes all that is really desirable and of true worth in pleasure, and much besides. Happiness is genuine gold, pleasure but guilded brass, which corrodes in the hand, and is soon converted into poisonous verdigris. Happiness is as the genuine diamond, which, rough or polished, shines

with its own inimitable luster; pleasure is as the paste imitation that glows only when artificially embellished. Happiness is as the ruby, red as the heart's blood, hard and enduring; pleasure, as stained glass, soft, brittle, and of but transitory beauty. (*Improvement Era*, vol. 17, no. 2, pp. 172–73)

Along with 27 percent of readers, I didn't know what *verdigris* meant, so I looked it up: "Basic copper acetate, formed as minute pale green or bright blue crystals by the action of acetic acid on copper" (*The New Shorter Oxford English Dictionary* [Oxford: Clarendon Press, 1993], p. 3563). Is that like what happens when a ring turns your finger green, or a bracelet might leave a green shadow on your wrist?

I was interested in the pictures this idea put in my imagination. Genuine happiness doesn't corrode your heart, doesn't turn it "green" with envy or jealousy. It may be that happiness, among many other things, is the opposite of coveting. I have always felt that one critical ingredient of real happiness is contentment.

Though genuine happiness doesn't turn your fingers, wrists, or heart green, it is infectious. When you meet a genuinely happy person, your own heart tends to be cheered and lifted just by being in his or her presence. Has that ever happened to you? Have you ever been in a situation where a person's merry heart really has done good things for your soul?

I learned an important lesson about happiness from Elder Jacob de Jager, also known as "The Happy Dutchman." He visited us missionaries when I was serving in Indonesia, and he used to say, with great joy and enthusiasm, "Be of good cheer! It is not a suggestion, it is a commandment!" My experience teaches me that he's right. The phrase "be of good cheer" and variations of it appear all through the scriptures:

"Cheer up your hearts" (2 Nephi 10:23).

"Be of good cheer; thy sins be forgiven thee" (Matthew 9:2).

"Be of good cheer; I have overcome the world" (John 16:33).

"Lift up your head and be of good cheer" (3 Nephi 1:13).

"Be of good cheer, little children" (D&C 61:36).

"A merry heart maketh a cheerful countenance" (Proverbs 15:13).

"Be of good cheer, and do not fear" (D&C 68:6).

"Be of good cheer, for I will lead you along" (D&C 78:18).

"Let us cheerfully do all things" (D&C 123:17).

"A merry heart doeth good like a medicine" (Proverbs 17:22).

Included in these wonderful phrases seem to be some lessons. One is that we have many reasons to be happy, such as the fact—the *fact*—that the Savior has overcome the world (and worldliness) and will lead us along. We're also taught that when our sins are forgiven, which is possible because of the Savior, we can be of good cheer.

Another lesson is that our happiness—our good cheer—will make a difference in our countenances. I have noticed this as I have met people who are happy and cheerful: They have peaceful, joyful, inviting countenances. They are the kind of people I want and like to be around. They're like happifying magnets!

Another lesson we can learn is that our happy, merry hearts will do good like medicine. Have you ever wanted to do something for someone who was discouraged or heavily burdened, but you didn't know what to do? Perhaps a merry heart—yours—would be just what the doctor ordered.

Based upon much thought, study, and many observations, I've come up with several essential ingredients for happiness. They come close to being synonymous with being happy. I've mentioned them in other places, but I want to group them together here. They include contentment, peace, serenity, grace, pure love, service, forgiveness, hope, simplicity, joy, a clear conscience, spirituality, reverence, and gratitude. There are many other ingredients, of course, but these seem to me to be some of the major ones.

Our prophets and leaders have given us additional insights. Brigham Young asked, "What will give a man joy? That which will give him peace" (*Discourses of Brigham Young*, ed. John A. Widtsoe [Salt Lake City: Deseret Book, 1954], p. 235). And David O. McKay explained an important source of peace: "The first condition of happiness is a clear conscience" (*Gospel Ideals* [Salt Lake City: Improvement Era, 1953], p. 498).

President Marion G. Romney said: "The key to happiness is to get the Spirit and keep it" (Conference Report, October 1961, p. 61). And President George Albert Smith taught, "When man is industrious and righteous, then is he happy" (Conference Report, October 1896, p. 71).

Clearly, there are many different ingredients that can help us to find and keep happiness.

And the opposite of happiness? The opposite of happiness is connected with the plan that didn't "win" in our premortal experience: misery. Words often used in connection with this plan are *darkness*, *chains*, *hell*, and *bondage*. The same plan is around today, and those connected with it, particularly the "father of misery," Satan, continue to try to get us to change our minds, our direction, and our goal of happiness. They can't stand to see us happy—not when they are and will forever be miserable. Haven't we heard so often that misery loves company?

I would like those who read this book to discover some new ways (and be reminded of "tried and true" ways) to recognize, create, enjoy, and share happiness. I would like to help us come closer to the definitions of happiness—closer to felicity, blessedness, and gladness, with a pleasant spirit of harmony and mutual goodwill (see *The New Shorter Oxford English Dictionary*, p. 1187).

I am convinced that we should be the happiest of all people. In this book I have tried to share something about *why* and *how*. Enjoy! Here's to your happiness!

Chapter 2

THE GREAT PLAN OF HAPPINESS

THE PLAN OF OUR HEAVENLY FATHER is referred to in a variety of ways. Among other things, we call it the plan of salvation, the plan of redemption, and the plan of reconciliation, but my favorite name for it is the *great plan of happiness*. I like the way it sounds and feels to know that there is a *plan* that will lead us to *happiness*.

One of the most important promises our Heavenly Father has made to us is that we can be happy both now and forever. There are many ways by which I am made aware that He wants this for me and all of His children. He shared a positive, powerful message through His prophet King Benjamin in Mosiah 2:41:

> And moreover, I would desire that ye should consider on the blessed and happy state of those that keep the commandments of God. For behold, they are blessed in all things, both temporal and spiritual; and if they hold out faithful to the end they are received into heaven, that thereby they may dwell with God in a state of never-ending happiness. O remember, remember that these things are true; for the Lord God hath spoken it.

As I think of the message of this scripture, I feel as if King Benjamin is asking me to look around and observe the contentment—"the blessed and happy state"—of those who are doing their best to keep the commandments. They are blessed in all things, "both temporal and spiritual." That reminds me of a phrase from a song: "Who could ask for anything more!" It brings me a feeling of fulness, as in fulness of the gospel.

King Benjamin then invites us to *remember* that what he has shared is true because God has spoken it. God doesn't break His promises. I am convinced that my Heavenly Father has never asked me to do something that was not designed to make me happy ultimately.

Many other scriptures and words of the prophets teach and remind us that the purpose of our Heavenly Father's plan is to help us be happy here and now as well as eternally. One of my favorites is from the Prophet Joseph Smith: "Happiness is the object and design of our existence; and will be the end thereof, if we pursue the path that leads to it; and this path is virtue, uprightness, faithfulness, holiness, and keeping all the commandments of God" (*Teachings of the Prophet Joseph Smith*, sel. Joseph Fielding Smith [Salt Lake City: Deseret Book, 1976], pp. 255–56).

The words *object* and *design* seem carefully chosen. They imply that happiness is one of the main reasons we exist. Lehi taught his sons this same concept: "Adam fell that men might be; and men are, that they might have joy" (2 Nephi 2:25). We exist—we *are*—that we might have joy. God created us, and He created this earth and put us here that we might experience joy and happiness.

President Lorenzo Snow taught: "There is nothing the Latter-day Saints can imagine that would afford them happiness that God has not unfolded to us. He has prepared everything for the Latter-day Saints that they could possibly wish or imagine in order to effect their complete happiness throughout the vast eternities" (*Deseret Weekly* 54 [3 April 1897]: 481).

Complete happiness! In our lives on this earth we seem to have samples and tastes of happiness, and sometimes we get frustrated because we don't always know how to keep it once we've found it. President Snow describes the kind of happiness that is complete and lasts forever, staying with us.

The Prophet Joseph went on to teach that "In obedience there is joy and peace unspotted, unalloyed; and as God has designed our happiness, and the happiness of all His creatures, He never has, He never will institute an ordinance or give a commandment to His people that is not calculated in its nature to promote that happiness which He has designed, and which will not end in the greatest amount of good and glory to those who become the recipients of his law and ordinances" (*Teachings of the Prophet Joseph Smith*, pp. 256–57).

There you have it! The plan of our Heavenly Father is a great plan of happiness! It is a plan—a plan designed carefully by our Heavenly Father—and not just a good idea or an interesting thought. It is great; there is nothing greater. And it does lead us to happiness—not just in a future time, but today, this very minute, moment, and inch of eternity. It is a plan of happiness, of salvation, of redemption and reconciliation. It is wonderful, specific evidence of the love our Heavenly Father and our Savior have for us.

Lehi taught the connection between righteousness—doing our best to keep all of God's commandments—and happiness: "And if there be no righteousness there be no happiness" (2 Nephi 2:13).

There have been times when I've listened to the negative voices on the news or read things that have made me wonder if righteousness was disappearing, if it was being squeezed out of our lives and hearts. If that were ever to happen, happiness would disappear right along with it. There cannot be happiness if there is not righteousness!

Throughout the book of Proverbs in the Old Testament there are many phrases tied to the following result: "*Happy is he* [and certainly *she* too]": " . . . that findeth wisdom" (3:13); " . . . that hath mercy on the poor" (14:21); " . . . [that] trusteth in the Lord" (16:20); " . . . that keepeth the law" (29:18).

And in the book of John there is this reminder: "If ye know these things, happy are ye if ye do them" (John 13:17). When I read this verse I am reminded that there are so many times in my life when I *know* things but don't *do* them, and I'm not as happy as I could and would be if I were to more consistently follow what I know.

The pursuit of happiness is a process. For me, it involves discovering what things happify me and then having the faith, courage, and strength to stay close to those things, making them part of what I think and feel and say and do.

President Gordon B. Hinckley has taught: "We are far from being a perfect society as we travel along the road to immortality and eternal life. The great work of the Church in furthering this process is to help men and women move toward the perfection exemplified by the Savior of mankind. We are not likely to reach that goal in a day or a year or a lifetime. But as we strive in this direction, we shall become better men and women, sons and daughters of God" (*Church News*, 6 March 1982).

As I have observed others, I've come to feel that we not only become *better* men and women, sons and daughters of God, but *happier* people as well. Happier and much more peaceful. Surely we can keep striving in this direction, becoming more and more like the Savior.

To me it's almost as if our Heavenly Father is saying, "Here's the way! Follow the map! I'll keep my promises! You *will* be *happy!*"

Perhaps the height of happiness—the ultimate in joy and peace—is pleasing God, having His will become ours, and ours His. No difference. No conflict. No difficult choices. This doesn't need to feel like a heavy duty or an overwhelming responsibility. Rather it becomes the source of our happiness: doing what our Heavenly Father wants us to do because we've figured out that anything and everything He asks of us is designed and planned to make us happy! It is the *object* of our existence, the *design* of our mortal experience!

President Gordon B. Hinckley is a wonderful example of optimism and happiness. He is like a "visual aid" for the happiness we can find and keep when our lives are dedicated to helping Heavenly Father with His work. He seems to have reached a point where his will is the same as his Father's.

President Hinckley has invited us: "Enjoy your membership in the Church. Where else in all the world can you find such a society? Enjoy your activity . . . be happy in that which you do. Cultivate a spirit of gladness in your homes. . . . Let the light of the gospel shine in your faces wherever you go and in whatever you do" (*Ensign*, November 1984, p. 85).

The image that comes to my mind is of us as Latter-day Saints everywhere enjoying our membership in the Church such that others are drawn to us, asking about the light of the gospel that shines in our countenances. They may be attracted to the peace and joy evident in our lives, even at times when we may have heavy burdens or challenging trials.

Oh, to be part of such pure happiness!—the kind that is so real and abundant that it can't be kept inside, but spills out into a cheerful countenance, a pure enjoyment, a genuine peace of heart and soul, a constant state of doing good and being good.

One of the clearest descriptions of true happiness I've found comes from Elder James E. Talmage. I love to read and ponder his powerful teachings about the difference between *happiness*

11

and *pleasure*—the contrast between that which is real and lasting and that which is only "pretend" and temporary.

In this day of counterfeits, adulterations, and base imitations, the devil is busier than he has ever been in the course of human history, in the manufacture of pleasures, both old and new; and these he offers for sale in most attractive fashion, falsely labeled, Happiness. In this soul-destroying craft he is without a peer; he has had centuries of experience and practice, and by his skill he controls the market. He has learned the tricks of the trade, and knows well how to catch the eye and arouse the desire of his customers. He puts up the stuff in bright-colored packages, tied with tinsel string and tassel; and crowds flock to his bargain counters, hustling and crushing one another in their frenzy to buy.

Follow one of the purchasers as he goes off gloatingly with his gaudy packet, and watch him as he opens it. What finds he inside the gilded wrapping? He has expected fragrant happiness, but uncovers only an inferior brand of pleasure, the stench of which is nauseating. . . .

Happiness is true food, wholesome, nutritious and sweet; it builds up the body and generates energy for action, physical, mental and spiritual; pleasure is but a deceiving stimulant which, like spiritous drink, makes one think he is strong when in reality enfeebled; makes him fancy he is well when in fact stricken with deadly malady.

Happiness leaves no bad after-taste, it is followed by no depressing reaction; it calls for no repentance, brings no regret, entails no remorse; pleasure too often makes necessary repentance, contrition, and suffering; and, if indulged to the extreme, it brings degradation and destruction.

True happiness is lived over and over again in memory, always with a renewal of the original good; a moment of unholy pleasure may leave a barbed sting, which, like a thorn in the flesh, is an ever-present source of anguish. (*Improvement Era*, vol. 17, no. 2, pp. 172–73)

Take some time to read these words of Elder Talmage again, stopping and pondering as you go, and I feel sure increased understanding will come as to why our Heavenly Father's plan is a plan of happiness. That which is part of this beautiful plan is designed to be forever, and thus the "pleasure" described and contrasted so well by Elder Talmage is not part of the plan.

Another important key to happiness is found in the New Testament: "Happy is he that condemneth not himself" (Romans 14:22). I've observed that many people seem to have an image of God being mad at them almost all the time. They seem to feel He is somewhere in the universe trying to catch them doing something wrong, and whenever they fail or sin it's as if they imagine Him making some kind of gesture or comment that indicates, "I knew you'd do it again! Why can't you be good?"

Has that ever happened to you? Have you had moments or even seasons in your life when you have felt that God was mad at you? Do you think He's angry because you're not perfect right this minute, and you haven't ever been perfect for too many minutes in a row? Have you felt at times that He's pretty consistently disappointed in you?

I have something to say about all of this: *Stop it!* It's not fair. Just because we, as earthlings, don't yet comprehend (let alone master) the concept of unconditional love doesn't mean it's not real. I'm convinced that even if you set a goal to make God mad at you, you'd never ever succeed. I think there is *nothing* you could do that would make your Heavenly Father stop loving you, stop caring about you, stop yearning for you to be close to Him, to come Home again and be with Him forever. He knows us too well, has loved and cared for us too long, to move away when we're "in process."

I have come to feel that God is pleased with us when we're doing the best we can do. This is an important concept in my life. Our Heavenly Father knows that some days are better than others. I love singing from hymn number 85, "as thy days may demand, so thy succor shall be." How kind of our

Heavenly Father to give us comfort, succor, and tenderness as our days demand. He really does know that some of our days are better than others!

A ZION KIND OF HAPPINESS

Many keys to happiness are found in the few Book of Mormon verses recorded in Fourth Nephi that describe the years of a Zion society following the visit of the Savior. Many times when I've read the Book of Mormon, I've been sad that there are so few verses to describe this condition we strive for. I would love to know more about a time when things were so wonderful that "surely there could not be a happier people among all the people who had been created by the hand of God" (4 Nephi 1:16).

One key to what happened in these two hundred years is mentioned four times in the twenty-three "happy" verses: "There were no contentions and disputations among them" (verse 2). I've thought a lot about this. I've wondered why contention particularly was mentioned four times when so few verses were used to describe these years of complete happiness. Perhaps contention is not simply one of the opposites of happiness but something that can and does *destroy* happiness.

The Savior taught, "He that hath the spirit of contention is not of me, but is of the devil, who is the father of contention, and he stirreth up the hearts of men to contend with anger, one with another" (3 Nephi 11:29). I had known that the devil was the father of all lies, but was fascinated (though not really surprised) to know that he is also the father of contention.

The Doctrine and Covenants offers this insight: "Satan doth stir up the hearts of the people to contention concerning the points of my doctrine; and in these things they do err, for they do wrest the scriptures and do not understand them" (D&C 10:63). To prevent this, Christ promises to "bring to light the true points of my doctrine, yea, and the only doctrine

14

which is in me. And this I do that I may establish my gospel, that there may not be so much contention" (D&C 10:62–63).

As we accept, understand, embrace, and live the gospel of Jesus Christ—the true doctrine—we can decrease and even eliminate contention.

Going back to Fourth Nephi, we read, "There was no contention among all the people, in all the land" (verse 13). Imagine that! Think just of your own community, or your own neighborhood, or even your own family: What would it be like to have *no contention?* And in this instance in Fourth Nephi, there was no contention *anywhere!* It's hard but wonderful to imagine such a place or such a condition.

Now we come to some explanation of why there was no contention for two hundred years: "There was no contention in the land, because of the love of God which did dwell in the hearts of the people" (verse 15). Here's an important key! No wonder Mormon urged us to "pray unto the Father with all the energy of heart, that ye may be filled with this love, which he hath bestowed upon all who are true followers of his Son, Jesus Christ" (Moroni 7:48). When our hearts are completely filled with charity, the pure love of Christ, there is no room for contention, unkindness, or any "cousins" of these words and feelings!

We read in Fourth Nephi that the church of Christ was established everywhere. Those who truly repented were baptized and received the Holy Ghost, and this continued until everyone was converted unto the Lord (see verses 1–2). Everyone dealt justly with one another (see verse 2). They "had all things common among them; therefore there were not rich and poor, bond and free, but they were all made free, and partakers of the heavenly gift" (verse 3). Gifts of the Spirit that had been lost from time to time returned, so there were "all manner of miracles" such as Jesus had performed while He was with them (verse 5).

One hallmark of this Zion society—this time of unity, peace, and happiness—was that the people prospered. In fact, they prospered *exceedingly*. Mormon described it this way in verse 23: "And now I, Mormon, would that ye should know that the people had multiplied, insomuch that they were spread upon all the face of the land, and that they had become exceedingly rich, because of their prosperity in Christ." The *order* in which those things happened is instructive.

They were industrious, including building cities again where they had been destroyed, even the great city of Zarahemla (verses 7–8). There were no "-ites," but "they were in one, the children of Christ, and heirs to the kingdom of God" (verse 17).

They kept the commandments, and they met together often "both to pray and to hear the word of the Lord" (verse 12). I love the beginning of verse 18: "And how blessed were they! For the Lord did bless them in all their doings."

It's tragic to see such a wonderful time come to an end because of pride, contention, separation, and, ultimately, a war that eliminated all the faithful Nephites except Moroni.

TWO PLANS

In the second and third chapters of Alma there are records of terrible battles between the Nephites and the Lamanites. The Nephites eventually won and established peace again, and in the process, a great lesson was pointed out:

"And in one year were thousands and tens of thousands of souls sent to the eternal world, that they might reap their rewards according to their works, whether they were good or whether they were bad, to reap eternal happiness or eternal misery, according to the spirit which they listed to obey, whether it be a good spirit or a bad one.

"For every man receiveth wages of him whom he listeth to obey" (Alma 3:26–27).

It seems to me this is one of the places in scripture where

the two plans are clearly defined, and they are shown to be exact opposites: the great plan of happiness opposite the plan of misery. And *we* are the ones who choose—we choose happiness or we choose misery!

When I think of it that way, it makes me wonder why anyone would ever choose misery! And yet I think that misery is often disguised—it wears the face of instant gratification, the appealing but disappearing counterfeit of real happiness. It seems we continue to make the same choice we made in our premortal experience: we choose our Heavenly Father's plan, the great plan of happiness, or we choose the other plan, the one that leads down, down, down to darkness, chains, and a complete lack of joy, happiness, peace, and light.

In this book I'm going to use the word *misery* in connection with the awful feeling that is opposite happiness. Sometimes we use it to describe how we feel when we have a cold or are sad, and indeed we may have little "tastes" at such times, but I want us to understand it in this context as a powerful opposite of peace and joy.

One thing that's miserable about misery is that we quit progressing—we experience "endless damnation," or, in other words, we become subject to the devil, as described by Abinadi: "[We] shall be brought to stand before the bar of God, to be judged of him according to [our] works whether they be good or whether they be evil—

"If they be good, to the resurrection of endless life and happiness; and if they be evil, to the resurrection of endless damnation, being delivered up to the devil, who hath subjected them, which is damnation" (Mosiah 16:10–11).

Toward the end of Alma the Younger's life, he shared some more important truths about resurrection with his son Corianton:

"Behold, it has been made known unto me by an angel, that the spirits of all men, as soon as they are departed from this mortal body, yea, the spirits of all men, whether they be good or evil, are taken home to that God who gave them life."

If we were to stop here, we might believe, as many do, that it doesn't matter whether you're good or evil, you'll still go home to God, and all will be well; but then comes the next verse:

"And then shall it come to pass, that the spirits of those who are righteous are received into a state of happiness, which is called paradise, a state of rest, a state of peace, where they shall rest from all their troubles and from all care, and sorrow" (Alma 40:11–12).

Alma goes on to teach Corianton that according to our works we will be "raised to endless happiness to inherit the kingdom of God, or to endless misery to inherit the kingdom of the devil" (Alma 41:4).

Imagine the difference between endless happiness and endless misery! It seems that this would be one case where the term *no-brainer* would come in. Surely it must seem clear that to choose happiness is the only way.

Alma continues: "The one raised to happiness according to his desires of happiness, or good according to his desires of good; and the other to evil according to his desires of evil; for as he has desired to do evil all the day long even so shall he have his reward of evil when the night cometh. . . .

"Now, the decrees of God are unalterable; therefore, the way is prepared that whosoever will may walk therein and be saved" (Alma 41:5, 8).

Alma seems to be emphasizing the fact that *we choose*. We choose light or darkness, happiness or misery, freedom or bondage, and much of our choice depends upon the desire of our hearts—what we think about, value, focus on, treasure.

And then comes this powerful, oft-quoted truth: "Wickedness never was happiness" (Alma 41:10). What a powerful thought! Samuel the Lamanite taught the wicked Nephites the same idea: "Ye have sought all the days of your lives for that which ye could not obtain; and ye have sought for happiness in doing iniquity, which thing is contrary to the nature of that righteousness which is in our great and Eternal Head" (Helaman 13:38).

If "wickedness never was happiness," does it follow that righteousness never was misery? Remember, I'm just using *misery* here to mean the result (the "reward," although it's hard to call it that) of our choosing the wrong plan. If wickedness never was happiness, then I think it is likely safe to assume that righteousness never was misery. Adversity, suffering, sorrow, and trials, yes, but not *misery* as it's described in the scriptures and by others.

In the book of Mormon, Moroni records what seems to be at the time his "last lecture." His father and all his friends and relatives—all the Nephites, in fact—have been killed by the Lamanites, and for all he knows they will find and kill him too. And so he is recording some of his deepest feelings, reaching out to us through the years to try to help us choose happiness and come to Christ.

Read carefully his description of what happens at the judgment: "And then cometh the judgment of the Holy One upon them; and then cometh the time that he that is filthy shall be filthy still; and he that is righteous shall be righteous still; he that is happy shall be happy still; and he that is unhappy shall be unhappy still" (Mormon 9:14).

Wow! It seems that to be happy still—to have happiness that will last forever—we must choose it here and now. We must seek, pursue, find, and cherish happiness. It seems we can't be entirely unacquainted with happiness and expect to have it fall upon us someday. *Now* is the time to discover it, to nurture and treasure it, to enjoy it, to become happy.

The opposite is almost too awful to think about. "He that is unhappy shall be unhappy still." What happened? I suppose, as difficult as it is to comprehend, that there are some who fill their thoughts, actions, and lives with miserable things. These become the desires of their hearts and their "reward" at some time of judgment.

They remain filthy because they've never repented or come unto Christ to be perfected in Him. They have not denied themselves of that which is ungodly (see Moroni 10:32). They have apparently chosen darkness over light, and bondage and chains over freedom. They have not been cleansed by the atoning blood of Jesus Christ. They have chosen not to live in such a way that they would be comfortable (and happy and peaceful) living with their Heavenly Father and Savior eternally. Ouch!

This is what Satan seeks. He doesn't just think about it, he *works* at bringing Heavenly Father's children into bondage and misery. Listen to the way it's described in 2 Nephi 2:27: "For he seeketh that all men might be miserable like unto himself." He will, it seems, do anything he can to keep us from happiness, and hope, and our Father in Heaven. He will try to convince us that there is happiness in wickedness, but as we learn the truth we know that this is impossible—there just *cannot* be even an inch or ounce of happiness in wickedness.

One of the lies of this father of all lies is to try to get us to think there is happiness in wickedness, and another is that once we've made a mistake we can't go back—we can't find the straight and narrow path again, nor can we ever grasp hold of the iron rod. He wants us to believe this, to become discouraged and hopeless because of our weaknesses.

Oh, how *different* the call of love from the Savior: "Wherefore, ye must press forward with a steadfastness in Christ, having a perfect brightness of hope, and a love of God and of all men. Wherefore, if ye shall press forward, feasting upon the word of Christ, and endure to the end, behold, thus saith the Father: Ye shall have eternal life" (2 Nephi 31:20).

What an immeasurable difference in these two plans, these two invitations! We choose which one to accept, a choice made possible by the atonement of Jesus Christ, as explained by Jacob:

O the wisdom of God, his mercy and grace! For behold, if the flesh should rise no more our spirits must become sub-ject to that angel who fell from before the presence of the Eternal God, and became the devil, to rise no more.

And our spirits must have become like unto him, and we become devils, angels to a devil, to be shut out from the presence of our God, and to remain with the father of lies, in misery, like unto himself. . . .

O how great the goodness of our God, who prepareth a way for our escape from the grasp of this awful monster; yea, that monster, death and hell, which I call the death of the body, and also the death of the spirit.

And because of the way of deliverance of our God, the Holy One of Israel, this death, of which I have spoken, which is the temporal, shall deliver up its dead; which death is the grave.

And this death of which I have spoken, which is the spir-itual death, shall deliver up its dead; which spiritual death is hell; wherefore, death and hell must deliver up their dead, and hell must deliver up its captive spirits, and the grave must deliver up its captive bodies, and the bodies and the spirits of men will be restored one to the other; and it is by the power of the resurrection of the Holy One of Israel. . . .

And assuredly, as the Lord liveth, for the Lord God hath spoken it, and it is his eternal word, which cannot pass away, that they who are righteous shall be righteous still, and they who are filthy shall be filthy still; wherefore, they who are filthy are the devil and his angels; and they shall go away into everlasting fire, prepared for them; and their torment is as a lake of fire and brimstone, whose flame ascendeth up forever and ever and has no end. (2 Nephi 9:8–12, 16)

President Ezra Taft Benson taught: "The greatest test of life is obedience to God. . . . Opposition requires choices, and choices bring consequences—good or bad. . . . God loves us; the devil hates us. God wants us to have a fullness of joy as He has. The devil wants us to be miserable as he is. God gives us commandments to bless us. The devil would have us break all of these commandments to curse us. Daily, constantly, we choose by our desires, our thoughts, and our actions whether we want to be blessed or cursed, happy or miserable" (*Ensign*, May 1988, pp. 4–6).

My point is that *we must choose happiness*. We must choose righteousness. We must choose our Heavenly Father's great and wonderful plan of happiness. It will be worth it. As the Lord explains, "It must needs be that the devil should tempt the children of men, or they could not be agents unto themselves" (D&C 29:39). Our exercise of agency includes *choosing*.

To summarize:

1. The plan of our Heavenly Father is the great plan of happiness.

2. Happiness comes from following what God asks us to do, from obeying His commandments.

3. Wickedness never was happiness, so righteousness never was misery.

4. Those who are happy *here* will be happy *there*.

5. We can choose to be happy.

Chapter 3

SOME WAYS TO FIND, KEEP, AND SHARE HAPPINESS

SOMETIMES WHEN I'M SITTING in a busy place, like an airport, I love to watch people and see if I can tell which ones are happy. It may not be fair—sometimes the happiest of people become discouraged, frustrated, and even angry when they're in a situation like missing their plane, having a battery go dead, breaking their glasses, losing their luggage, or sitting on gum.

But try it one of these days. When you're at the mall or waiting in line at the store, see if you can tell which people are happy. And see if you can cheer someone up with almost no "blip" on your battery by sharing a smile or a friendly "hello." Meanwhile, think about your own life. What makes *you* happy? I'd love to know, and have asked this question of so many (and appreciate the contributions). I hope that as I share a few ideas, I might include some of your favorites. But I also hope there may come into your mind some fresh, new ideas, or at least some reminders of things you might do to recognize or create happiness in your heart, your home, and your life.

MONEY

When I ask people the question, "What makes you happy?" I often hear, "Money!" Interestingly, most usually laugh or at least smile when they say this. It's as if they know, either from personal experience or observation, that having a lot of money isn't necessarily a source of happiness.

I remember seeing a bumper sticker once that said something like this: "It's nice to have money and the things money can buy, but it's important to stop occasionally and make sure we haven't lost the things money cannot buy."

Brigham Young reminded us: "The whole world are after happiness. It is not found in gold and silver, but it is in peace and love" (*Discourses of Brigham Young*, ed. John A. Widtsoe [Salt Lake City: Deseret Book, 1954], p. 235).

I've known many people who had more money than I who have been very happy. I've also known some, unfortunately, who seemed to have lost their bearings and their enjoyment of life, even their perspective. With some, a particular attitude toward money and "things" seems to have made them sour and selfish. Some have seemed terribly lonely, and have even said they don't know whether people are friendly to them because of friendship or because they want to try to get something.

I've known many people who have much less money than I have who are peaceful, content, and generous in their sharing. Of course, I have also known many who were suffering from not having enough of the basic necessities.

So I've listed money first among the things that people have said make them happy, but for me the things that follow seem to make more difference.

BEING MORE POSITIVE AND OPTIMISTIC

Here's an example of optimism: If I could save a dollar a year for a million years, I'd be a millionaire! And yes, this is naive optimism, perhaps, but you get the idea—optimism is a way of looking at things in a positive, cheerful way.

I am convinced that an important aspect of happiness is the ability to become a positive person—an optimist. This may seem like a "chicken-egg" deal: Which comes first, optimism or happiness? Does happiness bring a positive approach to and outlook on life? Or is it just people who live "the good life" who are optimists? (And what *is* "the good life"?)

My own impressions and experiences are that often when we say happiness brings the other feelings (optimism and a positive attitude), we're thinking that something outside of us is going to create our happiness. I think it's what's inside of us that makes us happy—our thoughts, the way we handle what's around us, and our deepest desires.

Sad to say, I've met some people who refuse to be happy. I don't know how to say it any better or more descriptively than that. It's as if they hurl their challenge to the world and other people each morning: "You can't make me happy!" Sure enough, no one and nothing else can *make* a person happy.

One of my friends told me about a *Peanuts* cartoon showing Lucy asking Charlie Brown what he thought this life was all about. He told Lucy he felt it was about making other people happy. Lucy then said, "Well, somebody isn't doing their job—I'm not happy!"

What about you? Are you generally a happy person? Let's say I'd like to get to know you better, so I find some people who know you well and ask them about you. What would they say? Are you generally positive, or do you tend to be negative? Are you more an optimist or a pessimist? Are you usually happy or unhappy?

Sometimes when I've asked this it's made people mad to realize that they're usually mad. They try to explain, "It's not my fault," and then relate some of what's going on in their lives. I think there are few (if any) people who have *no* stress or heartache or loneliness or other difficult challenges. The difference comes in how we respond to all that's going on around us.

For me, it's difficult to be around negative people too often or for too long at a stretch. It seems to drain my battery! There have been situations in which I felt someone who could always find the dark cloud was trying to pull me under—as if he or she couldn't stand it that I was enjoying the silver lining. And I, on the other hand, have been trying to say and sing (and dance prettily, of course), "Look for the silver lining!"

What difference does it make for you to be around someone who seems "dark" and negative almost always? Do you ever look on your caller ID box and feel like you're just not strong enough right now to take a certain call? Is your decision based on the fact that you can pretty much anticipate that the person calling will have something negative and pessimistic to share?

On the other hand, do you know people who make the world a better place because of their optimism, their cheerfulness, and their positive outlook on life? Are there some friends you enjoy being around because they seem to have a gift for making any day better? There are many people like this in my life—they're the kind to remind me that April showers bring May flowers. They are definitely happifiers!

Have you ever "thought yourself" into a bad mood? I have. And sometimes I've been able to think myself *out* of a bad mood! Amazing, isn't it? Maybe Someone's trying to teach us something about the power of our thoughts in such doctrines as "Let virtue garnish thy thoughts unceasingly" (D&C 121:45).

I've been asked more than twice where my optimism comes from, why I seem to be so happy so much of the time. I think I've found a clue in my response to football. Yes. Let me see if I can explain.

It is a pitiful thing to watch me watching football—or

almost any sporting event—"live," while it's happening. I can be right there in person, or watching a game on TV, or even listening to the radio, and my reactions seem to be the same: major stress! We're talking *agony*, folks! I scream and holler and shout suggestions (to players, coaches, referees, announcers, whoever). I can hardly stand the tension!

It would help if I could show you a video of MEE watching the Holiday Bowl of years ago when BYU played SMU and had a rather unimpressive first half. I was watching in my own home with a group of friends gathered around. We couldn't believe how the first part of the game was going. It was awful. It was even embarrassing. Here we'd gathered to cheer on what we knew would be a victorious BYU football team, and they looked about anything but "championish" in the first half.

Then in the second half they began to rally. It was an incredible comeback. I remember when Jim McMahon threw that 200-yard pass (my mother has told me a million times not to exaggerate), and there were about twenty-five SMU players in the end zone and only one BYU player, and he, Clay Brown, leaped thirty feet into the air and snagged that pass and the victory . . . I think my vocal cords were black-and-blue and swollen and unusable for days afterward. Events like this one have caused me to feel that I would likely die during some sporting event—I'd have a heart attack or something and just "pass away." (Get it?)

I want to contrast this with other times when I watch sporting events. I'm not able to attend or watch events live nearly as often as I used to. Other things have become more important in my life at this point. But I still enjoy a good football game from time to time. Many of the games I'd like to watch are on Sunday. I've decided that's not a good activity for me, based on how I want to spend my time and how I want to feel on the Sabbath. So I tape the games (or, if they're on cable, I ask someone else to tape them for me).

Later, *if the team I like wins*, I watch these games on video. It is incredible to notice the difference in myself. I genuinely enjoy the game! I'm not stressed at all! Oh, there will be those moments when I feel something's unfair or whatever, but generally I just cheer and clap and enjoy myself. "It's okay, boys— a fumble's frustrating, but keep on playing!" "All right, they got an interception, but that's not the end of things—hang in there!" It's as if I can say to them, "Keep going! Do the best you can and it will turn out all right. *I know who's going to win!*"

I find this is one way in which I can come close to explaining the source of my optimism: *I know Who's going to win!* Through all the sorrow, the inequity, the suffering, and the wickedness, I know Who's going to win. I know that eventually and finally truth will prevail and our Heavenly Father's plan will triumph. I *know* this! I likely knew it more certainly in my premortal experience when I voted for the great plan of happiness and shouted for joy, but with increasing experience here on earth I have come to know it again, and to trust that it's true: All that the Savior did for me and for all of us was not for naught.

Listen to the words of a prophet, President Gordon B. Hinckley:

> I stand here today as an optimist concerning the work of the Lord. I cannot believe that God has established his work in the earth to have it fail. I cannot believe that it is getting weaker. I know that it is getting stronger. I realize, of course, that we are beset with many tragic problems. . . . And yet I am an optimist. I have a simple and solemn faith that right will triumph and that truth will prevail. I am not so naive as to believe there will not be setbacks, but I believe that "truth crushed to the earth will rise again." (Conference Report, October 1969, p. 113)

He points out that there are many tragic problems. In my life I've experienced some myself and have been aware of many others. I try my best to remember that even when there's a fumble or an interception—even when we lose a yard or more—there is hope smiling brightly before us, and God is still in His Heaven, and Jesus Christ is still and will always be our Savior.

Our membership in The Church of Jesus Christ of Latter-day Saints gives us unending, dependable reasons for optimism and a happy attitude. This gospel of Jesus Christ is our source for a perfect brightness of hope. Because of the gospel, we are privileged to have confidence in our dreams of a better world and an eventual place of peace, rest, and endless happiness.

The gospel *is* good news! Faith in Jesus Christ, along with complete trust in our Heavenly Father's plan, brings to us a positive state of mind. Faith and the resulting optimism are like a "heart condition."

So how can you become happier and more optimistic? One way is to work to put a positive spin on things that happen around you. Look for the good and the uplifting in people and circumstances. I've heard friends say, in the midst of adversity, "I know I'm supposed to be learning something, but I can't for the life of me figure out what it is right now." Let perspective come. Do your best.

I once heard a story about a scouting party sent out during pioneer days to check an area ahead of the group. They came back and reported: "There are dead trees all over the place. There's a very small stream, and there are weeds six feet tall all around." A very negative report. The wagon master sent out another party to the same area. They came back with the following report: "There's enough firewood to last a lifetime! There's a wonderful stream that could be dammed to make a swimming hole! And from the size of the weeds we can tell that the land must be wonderfully fertile!"

HAPPY, THANK YOU!

I got to know Florence Richards well in August 1962 when I went into the Missionary Home. She and her husband,

Loren, were in charge there, and Sister Richards was like a heavenly cheerleader. She was *always* up! She'd write a whole bunch of happy, inspiring thoughts on boards in the large assembly room in the basement of the Missionary Home, and we'd take time when we could find it to record all those thoughts in our "IP" books. (That's what we called our books; I think it stood for something like "Instant Preparation.")

Although I've forgotten most of those little thoughts, there is one thing she taught me that I will remember forever. She suggested that when anyone asks how we are, we should answer, "Happy, thank you!" She always did that, and she *meant* it. For some reason that caught on with me, and I've done that since way back in 1962.

It's amazing how this one little thing can make me feel. Many times I've been just on the edge of Big Happiness, and saying "Happy, thanks," or even just "I'm happy," has almost always tipped me right into happiness. Maybe it's one of those "acting as if" situations, where you hear yourself say it and then you realize it's true!

I have found that it catches people off guard when you say you're happy. They like it. One day when I was checking in at the airport, the lady at the counter asked (without meaning it, I think, as she spoke with a rather flat voice and never even looked up at me), "How are you?" I responded, "I'm happy." Her head jerked up and she looked at me; then she burst into a beautiful smile. She looked like a different person!

She paused for several moments and then said with a tone of discovery, "Well, I do believe you're the first happy person I've met all day! What can I do for you?" She found out where I was going, checked my bag, chatted pleasantly, and even checked the weather for me. (I had never before known that they could check such information on their computer screens.) What a difference *my* response made in *her* response!

Once, when a group of missionaries at the MTC asked how

I was and I answered, "I'm happy, thanks," they said, "That's what you always say." I said, "Because I'm almost always happy." "But how can you *always* be happy?" I responded with something like, "Well, I've tried being unhappy, and I don't like how it feels!"

Doesn't that sound way too simple? I'm not sure. It just came out as a response to the question asked by the missionaries, but the more I think about it, the more sense it makes to me—I like the way *happy* feels!

I have to say that there are some people who know me well and now anticipate my response, and they "test me," so I work to catch them off guard. They'll ask, "How are you?" and I'll respond with something like, "Who wants to know?"

Try the "Happy, thank you," though, and see if it makes a difference for you. It just might!

LOVE AND SERVE ONE ANOTHER

There have been times in my life when I haven't been particularly pleased to hear someone suggest that to find happiness I need to serve others. I'm not sure why. Maybe when I've been a bit "down" or "blue" I've felt that *others* ought to be serving *me*. "Why doesn't someone make *me* happy? Why do *I* always have to be doing something to make *others* happy?"

But the advice is good. It works. My behavior can actually change the way I feel, just as the way I feel can change the way I behave.

What I have found is that when I reach out with genuine love and caring to help someone else, that feeling comes back at me. Almost always it's an instant thing, but there are also many times when the love and caring sneak up on me in an unexpected way an hour or a day or a week later.

Maybe doing kind things for others reminds us that we're not alone in the world, and that we're not the only ones who sometimes have challenges, heavy burdens, and cause to mourn. President Heber J. Grant, a very loving person, said:

"Make a motto in life; always try to assist someone else to carry his burden. The true key to happiness in life is to labor for the happiness of others" (*Gospel Standards*, comp. G. Homer Durham [Salt Lake City: Deseret Book, 1981], p. 161).

One of the greatest sources of happiness in life is to realize that we're loved, that others care about us, and that, as we so frequently hear, "we're all in this together."

COMPLIMENTS, GENUINE PRAISE, AND ENCOURAGEMENT

I was in St. Louis, Missouri, several years ago and had the opportunity to attend a small branch meeting on Sunday. As I remember, the Church had purchased two funeral homes in the downtown area and had turned them into little chapels.

The branch I attended had a membership of ninety-nine at the time, and everyone knew each other. I enjoyed that feeling very much. We sat in the place that likely had served as a chapel for the funeral home, and we had sacrament meeting.

During the meeting I noticed two deacons sitting on the front row. One of them in particular caught my attention. I don't remember his name, but it was something like Devin, so that's what I'll call him. He was wearing glasses, and he had on a suit that had maybe been handed down a little bit too soon—it was a touch too big for him yet.

It seemed to me that Devin was trying to be reverent. I noticed that he opened his hymnbook and sang, for example. I even noticed that he encouraged the other young man to be quiet and reverent.

When Devin was helping to pass the sacrament, he again was very reverent and respectful. He did things that became an example to me and helped me to have a meaningful experience partaking of the sacrament that day.

When the sacrament meeting was over, I found Devin and inquired as to whether I had remembered his name right. He seemed surprised to have a stranger speak to him and squinted a questioning look toward his mother.

I said something like, "Thank you, Devin, for being so reverent during our sacrament meeting. I think you're probably one of the best deacons in the whole Church." He grinned and looked up at his mother again, not knowing how to respond to this compliment. I think he could tell I really meant it.

I followed with several specific observations: "I noticed the way you opened the hymnbook and sang the hymns, and I saw you help your friend become more reverent when he started to goof off a little bit. I liked the way you were very respectful as you passed the sacrament to me and others." I don't remember what else I said to him, but I felt it was important to be specific and not just say a general "thanks."

After the three-hour meeting block, Devin found me and asked if I'd like to see the basement of this newly converted funeral home. Sure! He and others showed me the place where he said they used to embalm people, pointing out that it would one day be the nursery. Great . . . and very interesting.

He showed me the room where caskets used to be stored and displayed, and said this would be the Primary room. One of the adults told me that when the Church had purchased the building, there were twelve caskets left in that room. The stake president couldn't resist telling the members of the high council, "Have I got a deal for you!" We had a great time exploring and getting to know each other better.

What have your experiences been in giving praise, genuine compliments, and encouragement to others? Does it seem to make a difference for them *and* you? Does it help when you're specific about what you enjoy or appreciate or remember?

I'm convinced that everyone has need for such positive words and messages, and that Heavenly Father knows who His children are, what they need, and why. And He can help us be in the right place at the right time to help provide what is needed, be it a hug, a smile, or a word of thanks or inquiry.

GIVE OTHERS THE BENEFIT OF THE DOUBT

Have you ever been in a situation where you could really see and understand someone else's point of view? Maybe you've felt, "I probably would have done the same thing if I'd been in that situation." Sometimes that feeling will come from just giving others the benefit of the doubt, even if we don't fully understand.

We can give others a break by thinking such thoughts as: "I doubt he meant to . . ." "I don't think she planned to . . ." "I doubt they did that on purpose. . . ." "She probably didn't realize . . ." We can find a lot of peace in a lot of directions (reaching out further and further) when we give others the benefit of the doubt. BOTD! It can keep us from getting upset and seeking revenge or retaliation.

Part of what happens when we seek to give others the benefit of the doubt is that we don't judge as much or as instantly—we don't jump to conclusions as often. Next time someone's actions upset you, ask yourself honestly: "Have I ever done that?" "Would I or could I ever do that?"

HELP OTHERS BE AND FEEL SUCCESSFUL

One wonderful day at the Missionary Training Center I had the privilege of greeting some senior missionaries on their very first day. Oh, I know that first-day feeling!

We gathered in one of the classrooms, and I shared some information that I hoped would be helpful in the first few hours and days of their magnificent, holy adventure as representatives of Jesus Christ. One couple began to capture my attention. I noticed they had sat in the back corner and seemed uncomfortable. The brother, for example, was "fighting" with his collar and tie, as if he weren't accustomed to wearing them. My feelings became increasingly tender as I watched them during my short presentation.

At one point I told the missionaries that when they went to their first meeting with the mission president later in the day, they should take their scriptures. When the meeting ended, this couple waited until others had left the room, and then they approached me and asked, "Which scriptures should we take to that meeting?"

I remember clearly how aware I was of pleading with Heavenly Father to guide me to be helpful and gentle at this moment of worry and awkwardness for this wonderful couple.

I said, "Well, let's see what you have there." They had a brand-spanking-new "quad," the four Standard Works, in mint condition. I thought perhaps it had been a gift from their children or some good friends or neighbors. I said, "These will be exactly what you need." We visited for a few more minutes, and then they left.

I found myself watching out for Elder and Sister Jones. I wanted to make sure they were all right. I alerted my colleagues to their need for support and encouragement.

One morning a few days later, Elder and Sister Jones were in a class I was teaching. I don't remember exactly what the topic was, but of course I would have used some illustrations from others' experiences to let the missionaries know what kinds of activities might be part of their missions.

Once again, Elder and Sister Jones stayed after others had left. He had his suit jacket off this day and was fiddling with his suspenders as he tried to tell me what was on his mind. His dear wife explained sweetly, "He has a hard time telling what he's feeling."

And then the dam broke, and the tears came, and he blurted out, "I can't do this! I don't know anything! I'll *never* be able to be a missionary!" His wife held onto his arm and said to me, "He's really a good man—he's just nervous about this . . . and I am too."

I love the phrase, "My heart went out to him." It describes

exactly what I felt as I stood with those two great souls who were frightened of a new calling—of doing something they had never done before.

"Elder Jones, tell me about yourself," I said. "What are some of the things you've done in your life?"

He couldn't talk. He was trying not to cry. But his wife said proudly, "He's a rabbit judge!"

For the first time in my life, I was standing face-to-face with a rabbit judge! I told him that: "I have never in my whole life met a genuine rabbit judge! What do you do?" He began to tell me what it took to be a rabbit judge. Slowly but surely some confidence crept into his voice and his posture. I think this man knew every rabbit between Ely and Elko!

We visited for quite a while, and I tried to say some things that might help Elder and Sister Jones to know that the Lord was aware of all their life's experience and would help them to love and comfort and strengthen others.

They were much on my mind after that, and I had an idea that wouldn't leave. It occurred to me that many of the senior missionaries were going to places where they might need to know something about rabbits. I went to ask as many as I could find, explaining just enough so they "caught on." *Every single one* wanted to know more about rabbits!

I then went to Elder Jones and asked if he'd be willing to take about an hour and teach the rest of us something about rabbits—especially about raising them for meat, for a good source of protein. He grinned and asked if I was serious. I assured him I was. We set it up in one of the classrooms, and we gathered and watched a miracle. As he began to share what he knew so well, we learned so much! Questions were specific and meaningful, and he could answer with ease and confidence.

After that, all of us treated Elder Jones with the respect he deserved. It changed not just him but the rest of us too.

Every single person I have ever met in my life has had something important to teach me. Has it been the same for you? I regret that I have not always given every person the chance. But when I have done so, I've been rewarded in unusually wonderful ways! A great key to helping others be and feel successful is *recognizing* what they know and can share.

BE MORE SPONTANEOUS

I find that one source of happiness for me is in "connecting" with those who are around me. It's not easy. My tendency is to pull inward, to try to go through days and experiences without the scary challenge of interacting with strangers.

I'm not sure when or why I began trying to be more spontaneous, to make that connection with others, even if I didn't know them. Sometimes I've described this idea this way: "Do something every day that scares you half to death." I'm referring of course to good things, not anything destructive or unkind.

Do you ever have times when you feel as if your life is becoming somewhat narrow? Has it been a while since you've been stretched? Do you usually drive the same route to work or school? Do you sit in about the same place every time when you attend church or a regular meeting? When you go to the grocery store, do you move through the aisles in the same direction almost every time?

From time to time I've felt that I was getting into a rut—not a helpful routine, but a *rut*. I was doing more and more of less and less. My experience was narrowing. And so the phrase "Do something every day that scares you half to death" was and is a way for me to describe reaching out. Some call this "leaving your comfort zone." However you describe or practice it, it's a way to invite people and happiness into your days!

Who knows what adventures await us? Most of us are around other people during the day, at least some of the time.

Even for those who are homebound there may be opportunities for reaching out via the telephone or letters or e-mail or the Internet.

One place where I find it most challenging to speak up and reach out is on elevators. It seems like there's almost an unwritten law forbidding people to talk or laugh when they're on an elevator. Have you noticed that? Here is a group of friends, laughing and visiting, and then, almost as if they've been hit with an invisible wand as they step into the elevator, they hush. Everyone faces the closing doors and looks at whatever thing might be on the walls—like the last inspection of or by Otis, whoever *he* is. The "studied quietude" of the elevator is absolutely fascinating!

So I've tried for years to make myself interact with others on elevators. I'm sure my efforts aren't always appreciated, but often they result in fun and interesting encounters.

One day I got on an elevator and a man followed, and we were both using our good elevator manners, looking straight ahead and not speaking. He had some papers and was kind of shuffling them around a bit. My heart was pounding because I knew I wanted to break the silence in some way. I gathered courage and said, as pleasantly as I could, "Want to see my paper cut?"

It caught him *way* off guard, of course. I could see him fighting a smile, though, and I knew he was a goner. Once people begin to smile or laugh, the walls are gone, the pretense has fled, and wonderful things are about to happen. He responded, "Not really." "Good!" I almost shouted. "Because I don't really have one—I was just trying to make conversation."

Then he laughed out loud, and what a great time we had for the rest of our ride. He told me about a swell movie starring James Garner that all hinges on a paper cut! Apparently James Garner is captured by the enemy during the war, and they try to convince him that he's been in a deep coma for many years, and the war is over, and he's lost, so now he can reveal all that the Americans were *going* to do to try to win.

He must be about to spill it all, but then he feels his paper cut and realizes that it is the same day as when he got the cut, and he doesn't reveal anything.

What a difference as the man and I got off the elevator a few minutes later! We were chatting and laughing like old friends. I can't wait to see the movie.

See what you think. Try being more spontaneous.

WRITE A "HAPPY BOOK"

My friend Amy is good at keeping a Happy Book. If you live in Colorado and happen to know her, go see her and ask her about it. Her mother, Cindy, tells me she's been doing this for many years, and that it's a great pick-me-up when Amy gets feeling down. I think it will work for lots of other people too.

So how do you make or write your own Happy Book? You could begin collecting things that lift your spirits and make you smile—either quietly or out loud. Maybe you heard a joke that cracked you up; write it in your Happy Book. Maybe you see cartoons from time to time that hit all the right buttons. Cut 'em out and paste 'em in! Maybe you heard or read something in the news that touched your heart. Capture it the best you can and include it in the book.

I like to include pictures I've cut from magazines or newspapers. Sometimes I "doctor" the pictures so they make me laugh. How about cutting out pictures of people who are laughing? I have one I really like of little children playing with a hose, laughing happily, and it can take me to just such a summer's day from my own childhood.

You could include some of your favorite scriptures in your Happy Book—the ones that lift your spirits and comfort your soul. Maybe you'd want to include the words to some of the hymns or other favorite songs. Maybe you'll put in some notes you've taken of impressions that have come when you've been pondering or praying.

Try making yourself a little (or big or medium) Happy Book, and see if it makes a difference.

DON'T LET THE MOMENTS PASS YOU BY

Have you ever had a thought or prompting about something to do or say, and you got scared or distracted or ran out of time, and it didn't happen? Sometimes you will feel that still, small whisper—just an idea—and you don't want to let it pass you by. Don't miss your moment to smile at someone, to reach out and open a door, to pick up something that's been dropped.

We'll be happier if we learn not to let the promptings of the Spirit go unheeded or unnoticed. Can you think of a time in your life when your response to a prompting has brought great happiness into your soul? Wouldn't it be a wonderful world if God could always count on us? What if He knew that all we would need in order to reach out and help would be a quiet but powerful little prompting?

Consider the words of one of our hymns, "Let the Holy Spirit Guide":

> Let the Holy Spirit guide;
> Let him teach us what is true.
> He will testify of Christ,
> Light our minds with heaven's view.
>
> Let the Holy Spirit guard;
> Let his whisper govern choice.
> He will lead us safely home
> If we listen to his voice.
>
> Let the Spirit heal our hearts
> Thru his quiet, gentle pow'r.
> May we purify our lives
> To receive him hour by hour.
> (Hymns, no. 143)

40

What a wonderful source of happiness it is to feel and enjoy the companionship of the Holy Ghost! There is a noticeable difference in most of us when we are under that sweet influence. I've noticed that people who have learned to invite the Spirit into their lives tend to be kinder and more sensitive as well as more cheerful and peaceful.

RETURN

The book of Third Nephi in the Book of Mormon gives an account of the Savior's visit to the people on the American continent. Before He came, as a sign of His death, there was great destruction and death. Then, in the darkness, the people who survived—who were spared—heard a voice. It was the voice of Jesus Christ. Imagine how you might feel if you were numbered among those who heard what He said:

> O all ye that are spared because ye were more righteous than they, will ye not now return unto me, and repent of your sins, and be converted, that I may heal you?
>
> Yea, verily I say unto you, if ye will come unto me ye shall have eternal life. Behold, mine arm of mercy is extended towards you, and whosoever will come, him will I receive; and blessed are those who come unto me.
>
> Behold, I am Jesus Christ the Son of God. (3 Nephi 9:13–15)

What a tender invitation! It was not given to those who were very wicked—apparently they were all gone as a result of the destruction. The listeners were those who were spared because they were "more righteous."

But still they could be better, and He asked them to *return* to Him, and repent of their sins, and be converted, so that He could heal them. What a wonderful thing to contemplate! Our repenting—our changing, returning, and being converted—is part of the process of healing, of being made whole and well.

I remember a friend telling me about a journey he was making from Point A to Point B on a freeway one day, and he was in a great hurry. There was a section of the freeway that had not yet been completed. It seemed to him that they'd been working on it an awfully long time, and as he looked at it on his approach, it appeared that the only thing left to do was paint the lines. He reasoned that if he could get around the huge "Road Closed" signs and head on down the brand-new freeway, he wouldn't *need* lines—he'd be the only car on the road.

He managed that; he maneuvered his car around the signs and headed down the freeway, whipping along, feeling very clever.

But alas! As he got a couple of miles further there was a section of overpass that had not yet been finished, and he had to make a U-turn and go all the way back.

Obviously he wasn't the only driver who had ever tried this very good idea. On the flip side of the huge "Road Closed" sign was this hand-lettered message: "Welcome back, stupid!"

For me the little story illustrates a powerful gospel principle. We can make U-turns, or little turns, or any kind of correction, anytime, anywhere. We are not only allowed to turn around, to come back, but we are invited and encouraged to do so.

Have you ever made a mistake and had the feeling: "This is it. It's over. There's no way I can ever come back." The Savior doesn't seem to give up on us, so perhaps we shouldn't be too quick to give up on ourselves. And I *know* He would never greet us, upon our return, with "Welcome back, stupid!" Leave that to someone on the freeway. We are told that when sinners repent there is rejoicing among the hosts in heaven.

One of the most vicious and destructive lies concocted by the father of all lies (the devil) is that there is no return from mistakes and sin. He would have us believe that there are no U-turns allowed. This is *wrong*. We *can* turn around, change our minds, change our hearts, and come unto Christ.

In the *Bible Dictionary*, pages 760–61, we read:

> The Greek word of which this [*repentance*] is the translation denotes a change of mind, i.e., a fresh view about God, about oneself, and about the world. Since we are born into conditions of mortality, repentance comes to mean a turning of the heart and will to God, and a renunciation of sin to which we are naturally inclined. Without this there can be no progress in the things of the soul's salvation. . . . [We] must be cleansed in order to enter the kingdom of heaven. Repentance is not optional for salvation; it is a commandment of God.

I like that very much—a change of mind, a fresh view about ourselves, about God, and about the world. No wonder repentance—returning—brings such happiness to us!

One of my favorite hymns teaches this beautiful aspect of the gospel so well:

> *Come unto Jesus, ye heavy laden,*
> *Careworn and fainting, by sin oppressed.*
> *He'll safely guide you unto that haven*
> *Where all who trust him may rest.*
>
> *Come unto Jesus; He'll ever heed you,*
> *Though in the darkness you've gone astray.*
> *His love will find you and gently lead you*
> *From darkest night into day.*
> (Hymns, *no. 117*)

Can you picture the Savior, with pure love, coming to find you in the darkness and leading you gently back to the light? What a beautiful hymn!

One of the reasons we repent and return is so that we can be a light and example to others, a refuge from the storms that surround us. When we choose to try a little harder to be a little better (as President Gordon B. Hinckley invites us), we choose to be peculiar in a world where many take no responsibility for their actions and seem to preach a philosophy of "no consequences."

One day I was asking myself, "So, what's peculiar about *you?*" I wondered if I seemed good only when compared with the Wicked Witch of the West or Nehor. I wondered if it was possible to be "peculiar among the peculiar."

Is it unusual to try to be a little better when you're already pretty good? I think so. Can we be overly righteous or obedient? I think not. We're striving for *perfection*—for wholeness and completeness. We want to be like our Heavenly Father and the Savior. That's going to take quite a lot of turning and changing, a lot of striving to be even better when we're already pretty good.

Some don't seem comfortable with being unusual or peculiar in their appearance or behavior. Some struggle with their last minute and penny and breath to look like, behave like, talk like, and become like everyone else. Blend in. Not stand out or stand up. Not return.

I think about this because I don't want to become complacent or satisfied, to figure I've got it made and can coast a bit. I can't afford to coast. The many currents that would pull me downstream and over the falls make it necessary for me to row, row, row my boat and never quit striving in the right direction. I don't want to become "Mini Mormon," a minimal Mormon, always trying to figure out, "What's the least I can do and still get in the celestial kingdom?"

So the chance to repent—to change my mind, to go another way, to turn and return—is a blessing and a privilege. Is there something you'd like to change in your life? Would now be a good time? Come unto Christ, and be perfected in Him, and deny yourself of all ungodliness (see Moroni 10:32), and see what happens to your level of happiness.

FORGIVE

Few things can lighten burdens more dramatically than the miracle of forgiveness. Our burdens are certainly lightened when we are forgiven, and oh, how they are lifted and lightened when we do the forgiving! Our willingness and ability to forgive others is one of the greatest acts of love we can show to one another.

In the New Testament, Peter asked the Savior about forgiving others, and the Savior shared a parable about a servant owing a king ten thousand talents. The servant pleaded for mercy and was forgiven, but then he turned around and seized a fellowservant who owed him a paltry hundred pence and had him thrown in prison (see Matthew 18:21–35).

I've thought much about this parable, wondering at the meaning for *me*. Knowing how much mercy, patience, and forgiveness have been extended to me by my Heavenly Father and the Savior, how is it that I sometimes hesitate to forgive others?

The Lord taught Peter and all of us that we're not to forgive "until seven times," but until "seventy times seven" (Matthew 18:22). There are too many times when I find it difficult to forgive even once, let alone 490 times!

Think of how generous the Savior has been in your life. Think of the many times He and your Heavenly Father have extended Their tender kindness and forgiving to you. Think of the wonder of it—Their unconditional love for us. All that we have, even the very fact that we are *alive*, is because of Their love for us.

And then we might think of some of the insignificant things we have held against others, and the circumstances we've allowed to put distance between us and those whom we should love and watch over with tenderness.

We can, as always, look to the Savior as an example of everything we're learning. After being treated in ways we will never fully understand, while hanging on the cross dying, He asked His Father to forgive those who had been so cruel and unkind, because "they know not what they do" (Luke 23:34). Imagine it! He could have called down legions of angels to punish His tormentors, and yet He asked His Father to forgive them. Can we likewise forgive others because they don't know what they're doing?

Oh, may we become capable of freely forgiving others their trespasses and offenses against us, knowing something of what the Savior has gone through for us personally so that *we* might be forgiven of our sins.

Elder Jeffrey R. Holland wrote an *Ensign* article that helps me understand much more about why we need to forgive each other:

> Anyone can be pleasant and patient and forgiving on a good day. A Christian has to be pleasant and patient and forgiving on all days. Is there someone in your life who perhaps needs forgiveness? All of us are guilty of . . . transgressions, so there surely must be someone who yet needs your forgiveness. And please don't ask if that's fair—that the injured should have to bear the burden of forgiveness for the offender. You and I know that what *we* plead for is mercy—and *that* is what we must be willing to give. *Can you see the tragic and ultimate irony of not granting to others what we need so badly ourselves?* ("I Stand All Amazed," *Ensign*, August 1986, p. 72; emphasis added)

There are many other things that could be listed in this chapter about how to find and keep and share happiness. Perhaps you've thought of some as you've been reading. I hope that's true, and that you wrote them down and will do some things differently because of the thoughts and plans that have come into your heart.

Finally, let's not forget how happifying it can be to have meaningful communication with our Heavenly Father, to go to His holy house as often as we can, to read His holy word, and to see clearly to do what He has asked of us. May happiness come into our hearts and our lives, over and over and over again.

Chapter 4

A LITTLE BIT OF STRESS GOES A LONG, LONG WAY

Most of us experience times of stress in our lives—those moments so well illustrated by the poster you may have seen of the startled cat whose fur is flying in every direction, making it look a little more like a porcupine than a kitty.

I don't claim to be an expert on what stress is or what to do about it, but I *have* had enough experience to know something about my own response to stress, and I've observed and asked many others how they deal with it. And so I hope the ideas shared in this chapter will help you to do some specific things that may shorten the time and effort it takes to get from stress back to happiness.

Have you ever had a moment in your life when you felt like shouting, "I've had it! I *quit!*" loud enough for sailors at sea to hear you? Do you sometimes feel burned out, stressed out, emptied out, and just plain weary? Maybe you feel, as I do, that a little bit of stress goes a long, long way.

Are there days when it seems as if everything and everyone has ganged up on you? Maybe you feel like you're playing foot-ball, and everyone has "piled on." You can hardly breathe. It's the phone ringing (with people selling something you don't want and have never wanted), and someone at the door asking you to donate to the NAPP (National Association for the Preservation of Pigs), and one of your little ones telling you he stuck a bean in his nose, and the kitchen faucet still dripping, and you not having read your scriptures yet this morning because you couldn't find them, and . . . well, you get the picture (and it isn't a pretty one).

What *is* stress? Simply put, I suppose it's our reaction to what's happening around us. Often stress is felt when too much is happening, at least when too much is happening all at once. Although I can't believe that we were meant to be "stressed out" almost all the time, it is true that some stress is probably part of any normal life.

There are actually people who are motivated by stress, who seem to perform at peak efficiency when the deadline is upon them or they're surrounded by too much to do. Maybe they relish the challenge of making sense and order of chaos and coming out on top.

You may have experienced this at least once or twice in your life. Did you ever find yourself getting down to serious work on a term paper the night before it was due? Did you ever cram for a test? Did you ever plan for your part on the reunion program on the way to the park while someone else drove? Did you ever frantically grab everything that didn't belong in the living room and shove it in closets and bedrooms just before the guests arrived? (I picture most of these scenes accompanied by frantic classical music playing in the background, like in a cartoon where Bugs Bunny is being chased by Elmer Fudd, or Tweety is being stalked by Sylvester.)

I've watched people handle stress in a variety of circumstances: patients and families in hospital settings, missionaries and loved ones at the Missionary Training Center, drivers in the fast lane, drivers in a traffic jam, drivers behind a slow tank (but enough about drivers for now), people in line at the bank, parents with little children at the grocery store, teenagers before a date, airline employees on the day the airport shut down because of snow, travelers at the airport on the day the snow came, and so on. It seems to me that the people who handle stress well are those who are able to relax between one challenge and the next one. And some of us aren't able to do that very well, if at all.

Sometimes we anticipate stressful experiences that never actually happen. Was it Will Rogers or Roy Rogers or Mr. Rogers who said that most of the things they had worried about had never happened? There are times when we could relax but we're too stressed to do so, "knowing" something is right around the next corner.

We seem to be caught in what I'll call a "stress loop"—like a roundabout in the city on which we're driving our car, but we just keep going around and around, going nowhere, never turning off on the road to somewhere. Or it's like being on one of those twirly things on the playground when we were little kids, and we were sicker than a dog, but we didn't have enough sense to get off.

While I realize that stress is probably a *fact* of life, I certainly don't believe it needs to be a *way* of life. I've assembled twenty-three ideas about how to handle stress, and I'm going to share them here, mostly not in any order of importance or effectiveness, but just as they come to mind. At first reading, some of the ideas may sound ridiculous or impractical. But if they appeal to you in some way, give them a try and see what happens. For some of us, the more ridiculous or silly the solution, the more effective.

One caution: If you try to adopt all twenty-three ideas, it's pretty much a sure thing that it'll be stressful. Just pay attention to those that strike you as potentially working for you in your current season or circumstance.

1. *Find out what is causing the stress*. I'm putting this one first for a reason: I've noticed that if I can find out *why* I'm feeling so uptight and stressed out, I'm on my way to doing something about it.

Let's say you're having an SOS moment. (SOS stands for "symptoms of stress," of course.) It could be that you start breathing too fast, or you clench your teeth, or you feel a scream beginning deep inside your Scream Center, or you feel like punching the wall. You know you've reached some point of stretching yourself—your time, your brain, your patience, your energy—such that it's about time for a blowout.

One thing that helps me very much in such situations is to ask myself, "Why?" By now this is pretty much an automatic response to an SOS moment for me. The question will come into my mind, as if I'm having an internal conversation: "Okay, Edmunds, what's the matter?" And it's as if I can hear a humming sound, like a computer searching for a word or phrase, as some part of me begins to analyze what's happening.

Again, if I can figure out why I'm feeling stressed, I'm on my way to doing something about it. This may be helpful to you too. Try to figure out what's going on, and then you can try to decide what, if anything, you can do about the cause of your stress.

Can I turn off the loud music? Can I get out of this traffic jam? (Can I just leave my car here and come back and get it later?) Can I tell the person on the phone I'll need to call them back later (like in three years)? Can I turn the phone off for an hour or two? Can I visit or call someone and work out a misunderstanding? Can I apologize to someone? Can I soak my head in cold water? Can I start to sing the theme song for one of the branches of the military? Can I count dried beans? Can I organize my vast marble collection into tribes and family groups?

Can I step away from the edge, take some deep breaths,

count to 10 or 53, and avoid doing or saying something I'll feel bad about (and probably embarrassed about) later?

If I can do something about the source of the stress, I do. If not, then I work (yes, *work*, because sometimes this isn't easy at all!) to "step away." If it's El Niño, for example, I may not be able to do anything. Same goes for when it rains on my parade (although I could postpone the parade if I heard a weather report).

If the source of frustration is, say, road construction (think I-15 if you live in northern Utah), there may not be anything I can do about speeding up construction, but I may be able to figure out partial solutions, such as taking a different route, starting my journey earlier, combining trips and thus taking fewer, taking a bus, teaming up with others, and so on.

I can sometimes anticipate SOS moments, and thus make plans for how I'm going to respond: "Okay, Edmunds, you know the post office is going to be busy during the noon hour. Want to wait 'til another day to mail the package? Want to take some toys to play with while you're waiting in line?"

I may not be able to eliminate every irritant (at least not without being sent to prison for a long, long time). But by identifying the sources of my stress and reducing them where possible, I may be able to minimize both the effect and my response.

2. *As you can, take one thing at a time*. It isn't always possible to focus on just one thing. A parent with several children, for instance, may not have the luxury of focusing on just one thing, or one child, at a time.

But where it's possible, I think this can make a difference. Let's say I'm running around like a chicken with its head cut off. (I used to watch when Brother Jones would kill a bunch of chickens, so I know firsthand that this is a pretty accurate way to describe myself in some of my stressful moments.) I am *so* busy! There are so many things I need to do *right now!*

If I can, I pause, take a deep breath, and figure out what I need most to do and can do right at the moment. Then I stick to it and complete it, which helps me to calm down at least a notch or two so I can tackle something else. I don't always just do the easiest thing (although that may help me calm down a little); in stressful moments it helps me more to finish what I'm going to need first.

Let's say I have a meeting at 1:00, and I know I need to gather some materials for that meeting. If I can take a few minutes to do what needs to be done for that coming event, I can "unplug" it; my energy and focus can then be put somewhere else. It almost sounds like I'm describing the ways people work to get out of debt!

Perhaps priority is not the major concern in some situations. You may know yourself well enough to realize that if you'll do the dishes, or put away the laundry, or put a new roll of toilet paper in the bathroom, you'll begin to calm down.

For me, running in circles and trying to do a lot of things all at once just increases the feeling of stress. As soon as I can settle down, focus on one thing, and make progress, I begin to feel better. As a headless chicken, I'm not effective at anything (except maybe being a source of entertainment for others).

3. *Rehearse what you'll do when stress comes.* I've learned one thing for certain about stress: It will find you. If you're not at home, it will hunt you out in a school setting or at an office or other place of work. The printer will quit working just as you're in the middle of a critical project. The copier will jam or be out of toner. The library book you need will already be checked out. The line you get in will move slower than the others. The person ahead of you at the airport will set off the alarm and you'll have to wait while he takes thirteen pounds of metal stuff out of eleven pockets. A person from another cubicle will drop by for one of her seventeen-minute "sharing times" as you're rushing to meet a deadline.

Once I was shopping a little before Christmas and had quite a few things in my basket, and the electricity went off. No kidding—a huge store, and the power goes off! We all had to leave, abandoning our planned purchases because the employees weren't able to do anything the "old-fashioned" way, so we couldn't check out.

Knowing that those unexpected stresses will inevitably hit, it helps me to have plans for how I'll respond when they do. I can even practice, trying out different things to see what works best. I can make a list, kind of like a menu, of things that can help me pull out of the stress nosedive and tackle the SOS moments.

One reason for having more than one idea is that "Plan A," which worked so well last time, just may not cut it for this time. So you've got to have some other plans at the ready. When you realize you left groceries in the trunk all night and some things got too warm, dancing with a broom may not help as well as it did when you turned all the white underwear gray by accidentally including a black shirt in the load.

One thing I've already mentioned is almost always effective for me: When I feel stress coming on, my "Plan A" is to immediately try to figure out what's causing it. Another strategy on my "Plan A" list is to step back, even literally sometimes, and ask, "What, if anything, can I do about this?" So I've just found two bills that were hidden in a stack of Christmas catalogues and thus have not been paid and they're overdue. What can I do?

Those who know something about my personality will understand this next one: Still another part of my "Plan A" is to ask myself, "Can I just laugh about this?" Many times the answer will be "yes," especially if the stressor is something I can't do much about. Let's say I'm working at the computer, and I make a boo-boo and lose my whole document. If I were smarter, I may know how to do something about this, but as I don't, I allow myself a few minutes to dance around screaming, and then I laugh and start over. (Did I mention that this hasn't always worked?)

One of my friends has a "Plan A" that includes singing happy songs. Another says that music helps him too, but only when someone else (on the radio or a tape or CD) is doing the singing or playing.

I have a whole bunch of things on my "Plan B" list, including a lot of silly stuff: "Pull faces in the mirror," "Count to your age" (this takes longer and longer as years go by, and thus may become more and more effective!), "Pretend you're a cheerleader," "Remember some of the things your friends wrote in your yearbooks," "Lip synch songs from the radio," "Play an imaginary game of hopscotch or jacks," "Count dust balls," "Find some chocolate." You've got the picture. What's on *your* list?

See if it helps you to look ahead, anticipating that stressful times will likely come (because so many already have), and have a plan of attack. Talk to the dog. Take a walk. Clean a drawer. Practice whistling. Memorize a poem. Look at cartoons you've collected. Rearrange the stuff on your desk. Balance your checkbook. Read a chapter in your current book. Take the newspapers to the recycle bin.

The most helpful ideas are probably those that can distract you from what was making you feel stressed. You just have to have things on your list that will decrease, not increase, your stress level. Keep your list dynamic, rearranging and changing as needed. Ask others for ideas; something someone else has discovered and used successfully may be just the thing you've been trying to come up with.

4. *As you can, stop what you're doing if it's stressful.* Change what you'd like to in your life as you're able to do so. One thing to remember is that sin causes stress. Repentance is a topic we could spend a lot of time on, but I just want to

mention some specific things a person can stop almost immediately:

If you're reading a book or a magazine article that you don't
like, you can shut the book or magazine. If you go to a movie
and you find out it's not the kind you would enjoy, you can
walk out. If you're watching something on TV that isn't good
for your soul, and you know it, you can turn it off. If you're
being unkind to someone, you can quit it. If someone has been
unkind to you, you can try to talk to the person, and you can
work to forgive.

If one way is making you frustrated, try another way. If one
way you approach someone seems always to end up in a shouting match, try another way. If you've been using overeating to
try to comfort yourself after a "crash and burn," try another
way.

Look for ways to make changes in your life so that you
reduce the causes of stress.

5. Say no to requests you can't reasonably respond to. Here's a
tough one for me. Why is it so hard to say no? Are we afraid
people won't like us? Do we hate to disappoint anyone? Are
we "chicken"? (Chickens are not the theme of this chapter,
although they may seem to be.) Do we not like to admit that
we can't do everything and anything? Are the things we say
yes to things we very much enjoy doing, but we agree to do too
many?

I have learned (again and again, if the truth be known) that
to say yes when I need and want to say no is to add much stress
to my life. This seems so obvious that I wonder why I have to
keep relearning it.

And it's not always clear which activity to choose, as it
would be if we were choosing between good (going for a drive
with a friend) and bad (letting the air out of someone's tractor
tires). Our choices are often between good and good, or "have
to" and "have to"!

I've heard the term *buyer's remorse* used when someone has purchased an item, maybe on the spot, only to feel frustrated (and stressed) later because it turned out to be something they didn't need or even want. This same phenomenon may occur when we say yes to something that later we realize we don't have time for, don't have energy for, or won't really enjoy.

What can help us? How can we reduce or eliminate the stress caused by saying yes when we probably should have said no? How about delaying our answer? That can give us time to think it through. Can we really tend the children? Do we really have time to go to the play? Would we enjoy helping with the shower? Is this week already too full to add a round of golf?

If we can ask people to let us think about a request and get back to them, we may be able to think it through and decide that the game of golf would be more enjoyable (and perhaps more stress reducing) than something else we had planned.

When I have to say no, it helps me feel less guilty if I can truthfully add, "I would if I could, but this time I just can't." My sister Charlotte taught me to take a more humorous approach: "My schedule is full. I can't handle anything else right now. If you insist that I do it, you'll kill me. So say good-bye right now." Sometimes I can suggest another person who might help when I'm not able to.

What about the times when you have to say yes and yet you know it's going to add some stress. Could you modify the request somewhat? Maybe you've been asked to take your sister's children for a week while the parents go to Mexico; could you offer to take them for two days of that time instead? Maybe we get ourselves into stressful situations sometimes by taking away others' responsibilities rather than offering to help. Offering to help and support seems different from taking over.

I'm aware there are times when you'd like to say no but you

can't. Just be aware of times when you *can* be gracious in declining.

6. *Occasionally, when you don't know what to do, burst out laughing.* A few weeks after my father passed away, I was picking up the mail at the post office and noticed an official-looking letter addressed to "Friends and Family of Ella M. Edmunds." Wow—that seemed like a message to survivors. Why would there be a letter like this when Mom was still with us, when it was *Dad* who had gone Home?

I was very curious, so I went directly to Mom's place and showed it to her. We opened the letter, and she had me read it to her. It began, "Friends and Family of ELLA M. EDMUNDS . . . We were recently notified of the death of ELLA M. EDMUNDS. . . ."

It was one of those moments when just about anything could have happened, including bursting into tears (my feelings were still so tender about Dad being gone) or even getting angry that such a stupid mistake had been made.

But what did happen was typical for our family. I looked at Mom and asked, with great drama, "Why didn't you *tell* us?"

The letter went on to say that "the exact date of death was not given. Please enter the date of death in the space provided below and return this letter to us."

My brother Frank suggested that we have a kind of lottery—each of us could put in $100 and make a guess as to when the date might be. Winner take all. He told Mom she could even be included if she'd like, and if she got it right we'd split her winnings among the rest of us. Oh my. To some this may seem an inappropriate or even irreverent approach to things, but it works for our family now and has for many years.

One thing I have learned to laugh at is my compulsive behavior. I guess almost all of us have some ways in which we're compulsive. Mine include lining up cans in the cupboard with all the labels facing forward (but at least I don't put them in alphabetical order like Sandy does), spending the most worn-out money first (Frank and I both line up our paper money in our wallets according to wear and tear), having books organized on the shelves according to size (but Babsie and Ray still use the Dewey Decimal System), and filling the car at the self-serve station to have the cost come out even (Carolyn will even let it spill over just to get it exactly on a "zero"!).

Are you the kind of person who has to put all the Legos away yourself because you must count them and arrange them according to size and color? Does it drive you up the wall if all the clothes aren't hanging the same direction on just the right hangers? Do you sneak behind your children and rearrange everything in the dishwasher?

I think we can all lighten up and learn to laugh when it would help us to do so.

7. *Once in a while, change your daily routine.* It may prove healthy to change some patterns that have become almost compulsive. Relax! Back off! Maybe this way to drive to work is a mile longer, but maybe the scenery's more interesting, or maybe there are fewer traffic lights. Ease up! Give yourself a break!

There may be some danger in this. One woman told me that she decided to try it and forgot to wear a slip to work! Change the routine, but don't leave out any of the steps, okay?

For some it may *increase* stress to change the routine. Maybe some people who changed their route to work or school or the laundromat would end up lost and be more stressed than ever! So use caution with this one.

8. *Cut down on things that "drag you down."* What is it in *your* life that takes too much of your time and energy and doesn't give you much happiness in return? Is there too much TV in your life? Are there too many unfinished projects? Maybe too many nonenriching books or games or phone

conversations? Too many newspapers or catalogues? Are there times when you focus too much on *you?*

Do you feel stressed when you realize you've spent more time in *TV Guide* this week than in Third Nephi? Do you feel your blood pressure rising when you think of how many miles you could have walked out in the fresh air in the time it has taken you to play this game on the computer?

Do you see your profile in the mirror and remember when you were a few sizes smaller, but oh, those doughnuts are *so good?* Do you know it would help save time if you'd put the keys on the hook instead of just dropping them wherever and then having to hunt for them yet again? Do you spend too much time being mad about something long gone that you can do nothing about? Can you think of things that are running down your battery instead of recharging it?

Maybe you could combine some of these activities so you feel like you're using your time better. Perhaps you could be sorting through a drawer or a laundry basket while you're talking on the phone or watching a favorite program on TV. How about listening to music or to books or talks on tape while you're walking, driving, or working in the yard? You could even make your own tapes of things you want to memorize, learn, or review. Many find that walking with a friend helps them exercise, have a helpful discussion, get away from the apartment, and enjoy the beauty of a particular time of day— all at once.

What could you combine, cut down on, or even cut out altogether to reduce stress in a measurable way for you? Think about it. Try some things. Imagine how good you're going to feel!

9. *Work on increasing your patience.* I said I wasn't going to put things in this chapter in any particular order, but I do want to put this section in right here because it relates to the few things that have gone before. I've noticed in my observing (of

myself and others) that impatience is a contributor to, if not a direct cause of, much stress.

Sometimes my impatience is directed at myself: "Why can't you do this faster?" "Why didn't you plan so you wouldn't have to come back this way twice?" "Why are you so slow?" Push push push. Impatience.

Many times I'm impatient with others. I don't think that's kind or charitable, so I'm constantly working on it. I'll use driving as an example, because that's something we're hearing more about: this thing we call "road rage." Sometimes impatience can lead to behavior that we'd hardly recognize. We might find ourselves saying, "I can't believe I really did that!" After we've cooled down, we might feel embarrassed by our lack of self-control.

I figured out something one day that made me smile: When I'm in a hurry, it's the cars in front of me that bug me—they cut in, they go slowly in the fast lane, they don't signal when they're turning, they trap me by driving right beside another car, and so on. At other times, when I just want to "smell the roses" and mosey along, it's the cars *behind* that cause the frustration. I think: "Why don't they just go around me if they're in such a big hurry?"

What can I do? Mostly the frustration seems to come when I'm in a hurry, because that's what happens to people in the "fast lane." It seems to make a big difference for me to leave earlier—even by five minutes—than I ordinarily would. Then I talk to myself. "Self, you're not in a hurry—remember that." I settle down and relax more. I'm kinder and more patient. I'm less likely to get in some kind of Grand Prix competition with all the drivers around me. One of the biggest blessings is that I can spend the time pondering, listening to talk tapes, planning things, working through something, praying, singing, or whatever.

Here's another idea: Cheer for the person in the car behind

you to make it through a green light—you'll discover, much to your joy, that you make it too! I'm not the only one who thinks of such weird things, am I?

How about those mornings when you leave about ten minutes later than planned to get somewhere important? Do you notice that there are evil spirits working all the lights? Just when they see you charging down the road, *wham*, here comes yellow, then red. Every time! And for only the second time in history, someone has punched the button that allows pedestrians to cross the street while traffic in every direction stops and waits. Isn't it *awful*?

One time when I was coming around the point of the mountain between Utah and Salt Lake Counties, people in other vehicles were bugging me. Maybe they were going too slow. Maybe they were switching lanes without considering what I had in mind (ha). Whatever the cause, I was frustrated. And then a distinct, important message came into my mind: "Edmunds."

"Yes?" I knew it was going to be something about my driving, because it wasn't the first time I'd received some kind of reminder.

"These people are not your enemies. They're very nice folks. Look at them. They're only trying to get somewhere, just like you are. They didn't get up this morning saying, 'I'm gonna get Edmunds today! I'm *really* going to bug her!' Settle down! *Be nice!*"

Do you ever exaggerate your motions when you're driving so as to point out to someone that you realize *they're* in the wrong? I was getting ready to turn left at an intersection one afternoon when a man in an old pickup truck was sticking out way too far and was several inches into "my" lane. Well, I would certainly let him know about this. (I'm having a hard time writing so honestly about this experience, so please don't remind me about it when you see me.)

I exaggerated my left turn so as to indicate to him that he'd made me do it, that if he hadn't come so far out into the intersection I could have made the turn much more easily. Then I made a mistake: I looked at the driver. And there sat the most wonderful older fellow with a very kind, cheerful countenance. Just as I looked at him, he was looking at me, and he shrugged his shoulders with his arms up and out as if to say, "What am I gonna do about my driving?" It melted my heart and changed it at the same moment.

You're wondering why I've had so many experiences—why I haven't been able to learn "once and for all." I'm not sure. Is there anyone else out there who, though recognizing the potential for increased peace and happiness, just can't let go "cold turkey" of some of the bad habits?

I have always been nervous about sharing such things with others. Sure enough, someone's going to read this book and then see MEE out on the highways and the byways, continuing to try to be a kinder, gentler driver. Please be patient with me. Thank you very much.

10. *Have things to look forward to*. Is this one that lightens your burdens and lifts your spirits? It sure does for me! I *love* to have things to look forward to! They don't have to be huge, either, like, "Self, if you'll clean out that scary room in the basement, you can go to Bermuda for a week." No, I'm thinking more of the little things that can make a big difference.

I like to look forward to things I enjoy, like reading. I can reduce the stress of an unpleasant task by assuring myself that once I have worked on this project for two hours, I can read a chapter in a good book. That gives me incentive and motivation.

Sometimes you can get others involved. Maybe you could ask a spouse to think of some "reward" for extra effort on chipping away at a mountain in your life. Maybe you're trying to break a bad habit or establish a good one. "When I've been able to do this for a whole week, how about if we get a baby-sitter and go to a movie?"

Having something to look forward to can broaden your perspective and help you not to use all your energy or other resources on the task at hand. When you finish folding and putting away the clothes, how about spending half an hour at the piano? When you get the bathroom cleaned, how about reading a story to one of the little ones? When you get through teaching all those busy little second graders this afternoon, how about stopping at a bookstore on your way home? After you've worked up a sweat on the treadmill for half an hour, how about reading the three letters you got in the mail today, or going through an interesting magazine you haven't had a chance to look at yet?

It may be that we can turn some of our "chores" into rewards. Are there things we currently have a hard time getting excited about that could become things we look forward to? What if we changed the time of day for our scripture study, or changed the *way* we did it, such that it became increasingly pleasant, and not just something on a list of things that we needed to "get out of the way." Could we do the same for our communication with our Heavenly Father, our temple attendance, our mealtimes, our exercising . . . but now I'm getting carried away. Don't try to do this all at once, but consider the possibility that some of the things we *must* do might become things we increasingly *enjoy* doing.

Now that my mother is a widow and living alone, I try to help her have things to look forward to, hoping this will reduce some of the loneliness or boredom or feeling of uselessness that might come as she gets older. It picks up my spirits just to help her in this way. I look forward to doing things with her, and thus we're both helped and hopefully less stressed. Do you know someone who used to be very active and now can't do as much who might be helped by having things to look forward to?

11. *Establish a few more traditions.* I love traditions. Established well and carried on, they can be like waves—they just keep coming. You can depend on them. Not all of them can last forever, but for many years they can bring peace, comfort, and a sense of belonging. I love to remember our pageants on Christmas Eve when we were all little and at home. I loved our tradition of putting a puzzle together during the holidays, and playing Monopoly games that would last several days.

I loved sitting with the family on Main Street and watching the ten-minute parade on the 24th of July. I remember one year when Ann and I were a little late and missed the whole thing! I love remembering when Dad would get out the projector and show home movies.

I love the tradition we have in our family to gather for events, from baptisms to birthdays, from missionary farewells to weddings, from funerals to cousins' parties, from the fall "apple festival" to our family council meetings. We can't all be there for everything, but oh, how good it feels when we gather!

I used to teach a class to the missionaries about strengthening homes and families. One thing I felt made a difference was traditions, the things families do that tie them together in wonderful ways. I would always ask the missionaries, "What are some of the traditions in your family that you have enjoyed the most?" Often the sisters would think of things immediately, while the elders would say, "Aw, we don't have any in our family." I'd ask, "Wasn't there anything that happened at home on your birthday? Didn't your dad or mom ever do anything special or unusual?" "Well, there *was* that red plate. . . ." And off they'd go! More ideas than you could believe!

Traditions to look forward to can help us make it through the days when we feel stressed out or lonely or sad. I love one family's tradition of celebrating the first snowfall. When it happens—no matter when—those who can will gather for hot chocolate and doughnuts. What fun!

How about celebrating an obscure holiday, maybe one that's generally celebrated only in another country (until your family joins in)? How about a tradition of visiting or writing in journals or singing hymns together on the Sabbath? How about declaring a monthly Family Service Day on the 10th or 22nd or whatever date of each month, and having it on your mind as you come to family council, where a decision will be made about what to do next and for whom?

What if you were to celebrate "half-birthdays" at six-month intervals? What if you had a regular date for the extended family to gather each year? What if you came up with a unique way to use the extra hour you get when you change from Daylight Savings Time? (Sorry about those of you in Arizona and Hawaii.)

Some families have great traditions in connection with opening a mission call, or helping someone get ready to go to the temple the first time, or welcoming a new baby, or celebrating the grand opening of any business in town. Some families establish missionary-related traditions, including sending unusual "offerings" to missionaries from the family or neighborhood or ward. Some have wonderful traditions tied to special holidays, like Christmas or Thanksgiving or Easter.

I live by myself, and yet I have some traditions that I think are absolutely fantastic, and they help me look forward in a way that adds to a positive outlook. This really helps reduce the stresses of a particular hour or day.

For example, I have a family near me consisting of a single mom and a lot of children. I have a tradition of taking something (usually about a week or two late) for each birthday, and I save stuff all year to wrap and take over for Christmas. Another thing I do in connection with Christmas is pack my car full of wrapped gifts and visit some of my friends whom I don't see nearly as often as I'd like. I usually start a couple of weeks before Christmas.

One tradition I really enjoy is reading the Book of Mormon once a year. I choose something to watch for or ponder each time through, such as the word *remember*, or the concept of a Zion society, or the ways in which people were brought closer to the Savior through their experiences.

What are some of your favorite traditions? Can you think of some that would happify your family and others?

12. *Participate regularly in activities that are relaxing to you.* Learning how to relax is a great help in reducing and even removing symptoms of stress. What works for you? My sister Ann likes yoga. One of my friends likes a long, hot bath. Some people go to movies to relax. Some go for a walk or a bike ride. Some hike or swim. Some stretch out in a hammock. Some close their eyes and return to a happy memory. Some are good at breathing exercises or "power naps." Some read. Some write in a journal.

I remember talking to my niece Wendy one day about how hard it was for me to go to sleep some nights when I was stressed out, and that counting sheep just didn't do it. She suggested I pretend to be an ice cube melting, and it works! Thanks, Wendy!

Have you tried meditation or pondering? Taking a mental or physical retreat from all that's going on around you can be very restful and relaxing. It can reduce stress. Find what works for you, and do things regularly that make a difference.

13. *Write down your feelings.* Does it help you to write things down? I've found it can reduce stress for me if I try to put experiences, frustrations, funny moments, discoveries, and especially *feelings* into words. Some people write in longhand, some use a typewriter or computer, and some dictate things for someone else to type for them. Some keep a journal, some write letters, and some may even write books or articles as they get rolling.

Some have found it helpful in times of high stress to record all their feelings of anger, disappointment, frustration, and rage—capture it all the best they can—and then destroy the document by pushing *delete* on the computer or shredding the paper. It's almost as if the whole glob of stress goes away with the disappearing record.

There are times when I can reduce stress by writing a letter. It's as if someone's listening—someone cares about what I'm experiencing and feeling. Some of the letters get sent, and some never do, yet they all can help me get over the present trial or anguish.

When my dad died, it hit me hard. I didn't know how to handle it. Because I live alone, many of my moments of weeping and missing him have been private experiences. I have prayed hard for the ability to remember how happy and busy my father must be with the return of youthful strength and energy and many new, meaningful assignments.

One morning at 2:30 it was as if he awakened me. I had been trying to write a chapter for a Christmas book, and I had thought I'd like to write about Dad going Home just after Christmas, but I hadn't been able to get even a good start. But on this quiet, early morning, it was as if Dad said, "Sweetie, get up and turn on your computer—let's write a chapter." For about four hours I sat sobbing and typing, pouring out my memory of what had happened a few weeks earlier as we said good-bye to our dear daddy. It was a tender, holy, healing experience for me. I'll never forget it.

And by the way, my dad kept a journal almost every day for seventy-five years. Can you imagine what a gift and treasure this is?

Not all of the writing you do will be for others to read and share, but some of it may make all the difference in the lives of others. Give it a try: See what writing things down can do to unstress and happify you.

14. *Surround yourself with good music.* Are there times when

music can make a difference for you? For me there is music that is calming and soothing, music that is motivating, music that tenderizes me, and even music that drives me crazy.

When I say "good music," I recognize that we have a wide variety of tastes. I tend to like classical music best, but there are even some classical pieces that I consider "blender music"—as if the composer tossed a bunch of notes in a mixer and turned the thing on *high*, and the wild and frantic sounds are the result. If I don't turn this kind of stuff off, my stress level skyrockets!

Some people like jazz, some country, some rock 'n' roll or oldies, and some pretty much stay with religious or what they'd call sacred music—hymns and gospel songs. What happens when you live with others and there are three or four or eight different ideas of what kind of music is best to decrease stress? Yikes. Maybe this will be an important topic for negotiation.

There may be some creative ways you can work with different preferences. Individuals may need to make decisions about what to listen to and when, depending on the effect their choices have on others. Parents—and children—may decide that certain types of music, for whatever reason, won't be in their home ever. But even within those guidelines, people won't always agree on music choices. Maybe when someone is playing music you can't stand, you can choose to exercise or iron clothing or change the oil in the car or take a hike. (You may be *asked* to take a hike if you complain too loudly about what someone else has chosen to listen to.)

15. *Have a group of friends on whom you can depend.* Oh, what a difference it can make in your life to have good friends! I've thought of this in the different seasons of my life and have been so grateful to have friends who have shared the highs, the lows, and all the in-betweens.

Good friends are the kind of people you can be far away from for months or even years, and when you get together again you pick up where you left off. It's as if miles and years can't put distance between you and your real friends.

I hope you have some—those who know you well enough to understand the *whys* of some of your responses to life. Work to be this kind of person for others, too: a good listener, trustworthy, able to keep confidences, and willing to share time as you can, even when it might be inconvenient.

I remember when a friend of mine knew something that everyone wanted to find out. One person in particular almost insisted that she be told the information. (You could picture her putting her phone on automatic pilot after she got it, sharing the news in her whispery voice, gossiping her way into the night.)

Eventually my friend looked at that person as if in confidence and asked, in a low voice, "Can you keep a secret?" "Oh, yes!" the woman answered. My friend smiled and said, "Me too." Way to go! End of discussion!

I hope as you read this you are able to think of some good friends, even those you may not have been in touch with for a while. Why not try to reconnect with some of those people? True friendship is worth the investment. And don't forget that sometimes our best friends are also our sisters or brothers, parents or cousins, nieces or nephews, grandparents or children.

Finally, I think of the phrase, "What a friend we have in Jesus."

16. *Do something you've been meaning to do.* Okay, what is it? What comes to mind? Have you meant to visit someone? Is there a phone call or a letter waiting to be completed? Is there a certain closet you've been meaning to clean? Is there someone you've meant to forgive but you just haven't attended to it yet? Is there a class you've been meaning to take, a poem you've been wanting to write, a place you've been hoping to visit, a project you've planned to finish "one of these days"?

I love seeing those little round things, made of anything from wood to cardboard and printed with the word *TUITT*, that people hand out at Relief Society and the opening of hardware stores. They call the disk a Round Tuitt, and it's for people who keep saying they'll do something when they get around to it. Having a bunch of these "sometime" tasks cluttering your mind can sure bring a lot of stress. Tackle one. Grab hold and *do it*.

17. *Do some planning, some looking ahead, some preparing.* Anticipating upcoming tasks or responsibilities can allow us to minimize or even avoid the stress waves heading our way. Being continually disorganized and in a "flying-by-the-seat-of-the-pants" mode can be exhausting and very stressful. Some call this "management by crisis." Some even go to seminars with titles like "Dress for Stress."

Looking ahead can be very helpful. For example, writing things down can make a big difference. Let's say you've agreed to participate on a community panel about how to make neighborhoods safer. How about having one spot in your planner or notebook where you write down the ideas as they come? And you could flip ahead on your calendar to the date of the meeting and note all the details of where and when and why.

Let's say you have a lesson to teach or a talk to give, and you have floating pieces of paper in seventeen locations and can only remember where you put three of them. Again, how about having one place where you keep those notes, even in an envelope with the event, date, time, place, and topic written on it. Or you could keep the notes in the lesson manual, or in some kind of planner or notebook or organizer.

Much stress comes from trying to find things we *know* we've got *somewhere*. "Travis! Where did I put those warranty papers for this car seat?" Not only does our stress level go up but we also consume time that could be used for other things.

Once you've written something down, you can quit using up energy and brain cells to remember it. For many, this really cuts down on stress. They've written it down and put it where they can find it when they need it, and then they can get on with other things. I like to keep paper and pencil handy in several locations, just in case.

But don't get *too* organized (or you'll have to start laughing at your compulsive behavior again). Don't get too uptight about this "place for everything and everything in its place" stuff. Be flexible and strive for balance. Please don't miss a sunset because you haven't taken the lint out of the dryer, or a story your little one wants to share because you can't take a break until all the labels are put on all the file folders.

18. *Plan stress in your day*. This one's going to seem very, very strange to some readers, but hang in there. Try it at least once before you declare it stupid. The idea is to plan stress and worry into your day. Let me see if I can explain it so that you could try it if you wanted to.

Plan time each day for being "down": stressed, worried, depressed, whatever you choose to call it. Because it's going to be just once a day, you've got to keep track of the stressors—the things that are "bugging" you and making you frustrated. So get a notebook—not in a happy, favorite color, certainly, or it might cheer you up prematurely when you look at it. Get an ugly one. Keep it handy so you can write stressful things in it when they happen or when they come to your mind. The list might read something like this:

1. Dog not trained
2. Harold and Edith getting a divorce
3. I'm too fat
4. Apples have worms
5. Washer leaks
6. Todd got the promotion
7. Need to go to dentist
8. Hate getting old
9. I think Mavis has cancer
10. Jon forgot my birthday

Get it? Just write down the things that could take a lot of time right now, and then "let go," knowing you'll think about them later. I get stressed when I let things pile up on me. Making a list with the knowledge that there will be time (it's scheduled!) to get stressed, angry, frustrated, worried, and depressed later allows me to delay the stress.

Next, schedule a time when you're most likely to be in the mood to be down. I don't schedule my time in the mornings, because I'm a morning person, and I'm almost always cheerful and happy in the early morning. For me the evening works better; by then I start to run out of gas, and little hills turn into mountains. For you it may be just the opposite; if you're a night person, and it's hard for you to get going in the morning, that might be a great time to plan your stress. Your best time might even be in the middle of the day when there's too much going on and you need a "stress oasis."

Let those with whom you live know about your plan so they won't interrupt you. "I'm going to be depressed from 6:55 to 7:00 every morning, and I'd appreciate being left alone so I can focus. This is my only time today for being down, so I've got to make it *quality time*. Thank you for your cooperation."

Select a place. It's best if there's not a window, because little birdies and butterflies have been known to interrupt even experts. Sit in your place, get out your list, and *go for it*. Start with five minutes or so and see if that's enough.

Sometimes I get out my list and smile. Time has gone by, perspective has come, and I feel better already (without having used any time worrying or stressing about something). Maybe the dog ran away. Maybe Mavis doesn't really have cancer, or they got it early and she'll be all right. Maybe Jon didn't really forget my birthday and has a big surprise planned.

Other times I get out my list and things kind of cave in. I have a good cry, and wish I had a magic wand, and then I go on.

Often I think of my sisters and brothers in other places and wonder if and how their stress is different from mine. What would be on *their* list? I almost always come to the realization that I need to quit letting so many things make me so crabby.

Still, we have to deal with *our* lives and *our* realities, so give this idea a try and see if it might be helpful to you.

19. *Make a stress box.* I think you'll like this one. Have a place where you can "store your stress." It could be a shoe box or a used tissue box or even an envelope. Collect all your troubles. Have paper and pencil handy so you can write down things as they occur to you. As you write each thing down, put it in the box.

This is another way to delay your response to some of the things swirling about in your life. Of course, there are some issues that can't be postponed (without very unhappy consequences), but for those that can be, try this box idea.

So what do you do with those pieces of paper in the box? Schedule a time when you can take care of, say, three things, and just pull them out of the box at random and see what happens. Or you could go a whole week and then have a contest, seeing which item wins "Stressor of the Week." You could invite friends over to a "stress rally" and burn the box, getting rid of a whole lot of things at once.

These ideas are just some lighthearted ways to "stretch out" the stress, to delay it, to put it in perspective, or to help you handle just one thing at a time.

20. *Get regular physical exercise.* It has been said that regular exercise is cheap health insurance, and so it is—for both our physical and our mental health. Even short, regular walks can make a difference for most people.

There are almost endless varieties of exercise (and equipment—they never run out of new ideas, do they? Just watch some of the "infomercials" if you don't know what I mean). Swimming, running, tennis, treadmill, exercise bike, jogging, basketball, aerobics—the list goes on and on. The point is to find something you enjoy. If you don't enjoy it, you might have a difficult time doing it regularly.

And that's one of the most important things about the kind of exercise that will bring great rewards: It must be done regularly. I've joked that I *do* exercise regularly, once in the spring and then again in the fall. But what I'm talking about here is regular exercise, as in three or four times a week. Start now. Notice the difference.

21. *Get a good night's rest.* Most of us tend to have a shorter fuse, to get stressed and frustrated more easily, when we're tired. Don't things look darker, bigger, and more complicated when you're exhausted? Do what you can to get regular rest (not just sleep) and see what a difference it can make.

22. *Greet the day with a song.* I used to hear this phrase all the time when I was in Primary. I think it was our motto when I was a Lark. But I was also a Bluebird and a Seagull, and maybe a Pigeon, so I'm not positive. Wherever I learned it, I've come to recognize it as great advice: Greet the day with a song.

Maybe you won't literally get up in the morning and sing a song, but the idea is to start the day out right. Some say that even the first ten minutes of a new day are critical to how we feel about the rest of the day.

The Lord taught that the song of the righteous is a prayer, so maybe the reverse is true as well, that a prayer can be like a song. Prayer is a good way to start a day, especially if you include thanks. Maybe you can go out for a walk and have a song and a prayer in your heart.

Reading scriptures is another good way to begin a day. Having something that good to think about as you go through the day can make a difference. So greet the day with a song, a prayer, a walk, or a few minutes of pondering or scripture reading or whatever will get you off to a good start.

23. *Avoid unnecessary competition*. It seems to me that a lot of stress comes because of the expectations we impose upon ourselves and upon others. There is maybe too much about *winning* in our lives. We may be creating a lot of stress and tension through our inability to settle down and enjoy life because we're always wondering how to win.

Some of this comes when we're constantly comparing ourselves to others, especially Paul and Patty Perfect. Incidentally, I heard from an unnamed source that someone saw Patty Perfect being hauled away in a Patty Wagon, so maybe she won't be around to make us feel competitive anymore.

Have you ever been in a group of Latter-day Saints and discovered that you had the shortest patriarchal blessing? I have actually heard people comparing how many pages, and how many paragraphs, and so on. Imagine taking such a sacred document and using it to try to evaluate our worth!

Could we just settle down and not have to be best and first in *everything?* When I read Paul's gentle reminder in 1 Corinthians 12, I realize again that we're not all an eye, or an ear, or a hand, or a foot in this world. We each have individual strengths and gifts, and we need each other. Each of us matters to the well-being of the whole. When one member suffers, we all suffer with him or her. When one member is honored, we all rejoice with her or him.

So let Vivian have her turn in the nursery! Be glad for her! All right, so maybe you were convinced it was your turn. But here is a member being honored, and you can rejoice with her. "Good for you, Vivian!" (Sob, sob.)

Let's cut down as much as we can on the kind of competition that makes some people feel like losers. It's stressful when we're constantly competing over who has the most stylish clothing, who has more hair or a fancier car, who has the most spectacular visual aids. Let's work on cooperating rather than competing. So much about the world and worldliness tries to pull us apart. We should be pulling in the other direction: pulling closer to each other. Happification comes much more readily and easily when our hearts are knit together in unity and love.

"And he commanded them that there should be no contention one with another, but that they should look forward with one eye, having one faith and one baptism, having their hearts knit together in unity and in love one towards another" (Mosiah 18:21). It's a powerful analogy. As our hearts become knit together, it's harder for us to pull away from others, and harder for them to pull away from us. Hearts that are close have a tenderness that comes from the closeness. Once we know what's in another's heart, we are much less likely to be unkind or insensitive.

There are many other ways to decrease our stress. We touched briefly on prayer, which is certainly an important one. I love the hymn phrase, "Oh, how praying rests the weary!" Reading, studying, pondering, and applying the truths taught in the scriptures can help us handle the stressful aspects of our lives better. Going to the temple can contribute to a peace of soul that can carry us through many frustrating moments.

The gospel of Jesus Christ is a gospel of happiness and peace that helps us to live more joyously and enthusiastically—and more successfully. Our eternal perspective can shed a different kind of light on the daily nuisances, helping us to overcome trials that might otherwise sink us.

We are invited to cast our burdens on the Lord, and He will sustain us. Let Him comfort you, heal you, and bring you peace of heart and soul, as He has promised: "Peace I leave with you, my peace I give unto you: not as the world giveth, give I unto you. Let not your heart be troubled, neither let it be afraid" (John 14:27).

Chapter 5

ADVERSITY AND AFFLICTIONS

HAVE YOU EVER WATCHED CHILDREN playing and had "flash-backs" of times when such simple things made you laugh and feel happy? Do you remember floating sticks in the ditch, playing in the hose or sandpile, reading with a flashlight under the covers, sleeping out under the stars, trying to go to sleep on Christmas Eve, getting brand-new school shoes, having a whole piece of cake, going on a family vacation, or any number of other happy memories?

Some have not forgotten the joy of childhood experiences. Many still find peace, contentment, and gratitude in such simple things as a sunrise or sunset, a visit from a friend, the song of a bird, the smell of rain, and the sound of the wind in the trees.

Others are so focused on their own pain, anger, resentments, and fears that they cannot see any joy in life. They want to know (and it seems like a reasonable question): Why aren't we happy *all the time?* Why is there adversity and suffering? Why do we have so much sorrow in this world, and so many trials? Why do so many things seem so unfair and unjust?

When I have talked to people about the great plan of happiness, some have responded, "But what about . . ." And then they relate the tragedy that has come to them or to someone they know, and they wonder how such terrible things can happen—why they would be allowed if this is in fact the great plan of *happiness*.

One day when I was being a "frowny face," murmuring and fussing about one thing and another, I was trying to shoot holes in the notion that we *are*—we *exist*—to have joy (see 2 Nephi 2:25). Maybe I wasn't having a very happy time, and I wanted to doubt the idea that all righteous roads lead to joy.

But I made a good decision: I read the Book of Mormon verse in context. I kept going further and further on both sides. I won't take time or space to do that here, more than a verse or two on either side, but I highly recommend it. Read the whole chapter. Read the whole book!

Lehi teaches Jacob—and all of us—that "all things have been done in the wisdom of him who knoweth all things" (2 Nephi 2:24). Think of it! Everything is part of a plan, and the plan is about joy and happiness. Our Heavenly Father can see the whole picture, whereas we see just a little part of it.

Right after that explanation that all things have been done in God's wisdom comes the truth that we are that we might have joy. And then on the "other side" is the *reason* for this: "And the Messiah cometh . . ." (2 Nephi 2:26).

That's all we need, really: "The Messiah cometh"! But Lehi adds more: "And the Messiah cometh in the fulness of time, that he may redeem the children of men from the fall" (2 Nephi 2:26).

I'm not always able to pull myself out of my frowny-face moments. Sometimes I have, in my sadness, wondered if "they" knew what our lives would be like when "they" said that about joy, and when "they" wrote all those other things about cheering up our hearts and being happy and all. Did they know how hard some of our experiences would be? Did they know how long and lonely some nights would seem? Did they have any idea how heavy some burdens would feel?

They knew. They *know*. They understood and they understand. The fact is, *we* knew! We knew when we voted for this plan of happiness and shouted for joy that our lives on earth would bring us close to much suffering.

Elder Neal A. Maxwell explains some of our responses to sufferings and trials:

> If we criticize God or are unduly miffed over sufferings and tribulation, we are really criticizing the Planner for implementing the very plan we once approved, premortally (see Job 38:4, 7). Granted, we don't now remember the actual approval. But not remembering is actually part of the plan! In the midst of vexing difficulties, since we shouted "for joy" in the premortal world, sometimes we may wonder now what all the shouting was about! (*That Ye May Believe* [Salt Lake City: Bookcraft, 1992], p. 11)

There are many evidences that our Heavenly Father, the Savior, the prophets, and others knew that life would not be free from trials and adversity. There are even some indications in the covenants we make when we're baptized.

The fullest account we have of our baptismal covenant is recorded in the Book of Mormon (see Mosiah 18:7–11). Among other very important things, the covenant includes a willingness to "bear one another's burdens, that they may be light," to "mourn with those that mourn, . . . and comfort those that stand in need of comfort."

When the people understood these and all the other aspects of the covenant they were about to make, they clapped their hands for joy, letting Alma know that this was *exactly* what they wanted to do—who and how they wanted to be! This was the desire of their hearts.

I have thought that if everything in life was supposed to be smooth sailing, why would those phrases about burdens and mourning be included in the baptismal covenant at all? If there were to be no adversity in our lives on earth, perhaps the covenant would have had things like "party with those who party; eat, drink, and be merry; don't worry about anyone else. No tears! No fears!" The fact that we are asked to help each other in times of difficulty indicates a perfect understanding that life would not be without its challenges.

Elder L. Aldin Porter quoted the story from 3 Nephi 14:24–27 of the two men who built houses, one upon sand and the other upon rock. Then he asked: "Did you note that the rain descended and the floods came and the winds blew upon *both* houses? Just because we follow the word of the Lord does not mean we will suffer no ill winds; it does mean that we will spiritually survive them!" (*Ensign*, November 1987, p. 74).

Adversity and sorrow—heavy burdens—seem to be part of life, don't they? Dr. Norman Vincent Peale, speaking to BYU students on October 22, 1963, said that "problems constitute a sign of life." On that basis, most of us would have to admit we're alive!

I believe I was convinced for a time that if people were *good*—if they were prepared and righteous—they shouldn't and wouldn't even experience any adversity. But that's not the plan we voted for, is it?

When some conversations about life come to the conclusion that because there is suffering there is no God, or because there is adversity there is no happiness, or because we have heavy burdens it means that God is mad at us—that we're being punished—I am reminded of the many examples, in the scriptures, in history, and in life "right now," of trials and afflictions as *blessings*. Yes, as blessings.

I learn much from looking at the prophet Lehi's life. He had left an apparently comfortable home in Jerusalem, although perhaps by the time he and his family left, it wasn't very peaceful or safe. He and his wife and family had gone into the wilderness, had crossed an ocean, and had seen much sorrow.

His own sons had wanted to kill him. He had experienced so much suffering and anguish, and yet he still taught that we are here on earth that we might have joy! He *knew* there was much about life that didn't seem very joyful, but he taught that truth anyway.

It's also instructive to read the story of Jared and his brother and those who traveled with them to the promised land. I'm often tempted to contrast these people with Laman and Lemuel and the others who murmured and kicked and screamed all the way along.

The brother of Jared was instrumental in preparing barges in which to travel, and he counseled with and received extraordinary help from the Lord in preparing stones to give light and holes to let in fresh air. Then the voyagers apparently went through almost a year of "bouncing around" in the ocean, yet they didn't murmur. They seemed to know that this adversity would be but for a small moment, and that it was leading to some high and important purpose. Think for just a moment what that journey must have been like:

> And it came to pass that the Lord God caused that there should be a furious wind blow upon the face of the waters, towards the promised land; and thus they were tossed upon the waves of the sea before the wind.
>
> And it came to pass that they were many times buried in the depths of the sea, because of the mountain waves which broke upon them, and also the great and terrible tempests which were caused by the fierceness of the wind. . . .
>
> And thus they were driven forth, three hundred and forty and four days upon the water. (Ether 6:5–6, 11)

Imagine the terror, the physical difficulty, the seasickness! But did they murmur? On the contrary:

> They did sing praises unto the Lord; yea, the brother of Jared did sing praises unto the Lord, and he did thank and praise the Lord all the day long; and when the night came, they did not cease to praise the Lord. . . .

And when they had set their feet upon the shores of the promised land they bowed themselves down upon the face of the land, and did humble themselves before the Lord, and did shed tears of joy before the Lord, because of the multitude of his tender mercies over them. (Ether 6:9, 12)

What a great example to us!

As always, our greatest example is our Savior, who came to earth to receive a body, experience mortality, and go through incomprehensible suffering to bring about the Atonement, holding out to us the reality of resurrection and the hope of eternal life with Him and our Heavenly Parents.

Could we say that the Savior's experiences in the Garden of Gethsemane and on the cross were times of suffering? Perhaps we search for a stronger, more descriptive word than *suffering*. Even for His loved ones, in heaven as well as on earth, there certainly must have been terrible suffering of a depth and quality that we'll likely never fully comprehend.

And yet He taught, "In the world ye shall have tribulation: but be of good cheer; I have overcome the world" (John 16:33). He knows we'll have tribulation—it comes with life in this world—but He's literally "cheering us on"!

President Marion G. Romney taught that although we know life will give us experience with adversity and suffering,

> This does not mean that we crave suffering. We avoid all we can. However, we now know, and we all knew when we elected to come into mortality, that we would here be proved in the crucible of adversity and affliction. "And we will prove them . . . to see if they will do all things whatsoever the Lord their God shall command them." (Abr. 3:25.) The Father's plan for proving his children did not exempt the Savior himself. The suffering he undertook to endure, and which he did endure, equaled the combined suffering of all men. Eighteen hundred years after he had endured it, he spoke of it as being so intense that it "caused myself, even God, the greatest of all, to tremble because of pain, and to

82

bleed at every pore, and to suffer both body and spirit—and would that I might not drink the bitter cup, and shrink—

"Nevertheless, [he concluded,] glory be to the Father, and I partook and finished my preparations unto the children of men." (D&C 19:18–19.) (Conference Report, October 1969, p. 58)

When I think of the lives of our Savior and His prophets and others, I feel ashamed for murmuring, for sometimes thinking I'm suffering so much. And yet I *do* experience sorrow and I *do* struggle with heavy burdens. Are mine "nothing" when compared to what others experience? I think our individual trials and adversity matter, and that they are heavy and difficult enough to teach us great, eternal lessons. I don't think the Savior or any of the prophets meant to diminish the importance of our experiences when they shared their own sorrows.

It's clear that those who have taught about joy and happiness *do* know about sorrow and suffering. Maybe that's why they teach with such tenderness as well as with such power. Are there people in your life who seem refined and purified by their experiences with sorrow and adversity? What have you learned with and from them? What have you learned through your own trials?

Could it be that in some ways our suffering and trials help us to see more clearly the sweetness of joy and happiness? Some have described adversity's effects that way. Elder Neal A. Maxwell taught, "Righteous sorrow and suffering carve cavities in the soul that will become later reservoirs of joy" (*Meek and Lowly* [Salt Lake City: Deseret Book, 1987], p. 11).

Remember how Lehi taught that if not for opposition there would be "no life neither death, nor corruption nor incorruption, happiness nor misery, neither sense nor insensibility" (2 Nephi 2:11). Without challenge and choice, we would have had a very "flat" existence. In fact, that was part of another plan. . . .

And so we have opposition and contrast. And what do we learn? I've wondered how those who have spent years in prison camps (such as those who are prisoners of war) feel about freedom. And how do their feelings compare with those of refugees who have fled their homes seeking safety? Think of all such refugees through history—Abraham with his family, Moses with the Israelites, Lehi and family, Joseph and Mary with Jesus as they fled to Egypt, the pioneers, and the millions right now in all parts of the world who are dealing with such terrible, terrible suffering.

I've wondered what deep and lasting lessons have been learned by those who have been stranded in storms, on oceans, or in buildings destroyed by bombs or earthquakes. How do those who live at the "top of the earth" feel about sunlight? How do those who have never had a day without feeling hungry feel about a little cup of warm soup and a little piece of bread or bowl of rice? What can we learn from each other?

I have always loved a quote that was shared with me years ago at a time when I needed it: "In these days of sore trial, Christ our Lord is our Guide and our Savior. This is the thing that is giving us a glad confidence that all things are working together for good. So when the darkness comes, let us remember that the night brings out the stars as sorrows show us the truth: and the insight that comes through pain and disappointment may be the insight into the value of what we are" (Levi Edgar Young, Conference Report, October 1932, p. 59).

Christ *is* our Savior and our Guide. He and our Heavenly Father will be with us in every time of trouble. By and by, everything will "come clear," and we will finally understand the reasons for some of our valleys and heartaches, our anguish and our seemingly unanswered or ignored pleas.

In hymn number 85, "How Firm a Foundation," we find these comforting, instructive words:

When through the deep waters I call thee to go,
The rivers of sorrow shall not thee o'erflow,
For I will be with thee, thy troubles to bless,
And sanctify to thee thy deepest distress.

I think that's beautiful. God doesn't want us to drown—to be completely overcome and to give up. He wants to bless us in our troubles, and to sanctify to us our deepest distress. And the next verse reads:

When through fiery trials thy pathway shall lie,
My grace, all sufficient, shall be thy supply.
The flame shall not hurt thee; I only design
Thy dross to consume and thy gold to refine.

Most of us will pass through some fiery trials, but, as we're taught in the words of the hymn, the flame shall not hurt us. God is burning away our dross (that which is not Godlike in us) and refining our gold.

I ran across a Chinese proverb years ago that said simply, "Pure gold fears no fire." Perhaps pure people don't fear the fire either. They can't be hurt by it. The dross is gone already.

Remember Alma and Amulek? Nephi and Lehi? The three Nephite disciples who remained on the earth after the others had died?

How about Shadrach, Meshach, and Abednego, who refused to worship the golden image King Nebuchadnezzar had set up? They were cast into a furnace that had been heated so much more than usual that the men who cast them in died!

But because of their purity—the gold of their souls already having been refined—the flame did not hurt them. The king was astonished to see *four* men, one of whom he described as "like the Son of God," walking around in the midst of the fire without being hurt at all. (Read Daniel 3:14–26 and beyond if you haven't for a while.)

I'm aware that many who are pure and holy have perished in fires. Remember what happened to the women and children believers and their scriptures in Ammonihah? (see Alma 14). But I learn from these verses in the hymns, from other experiences in the scriptures and history, and from my own life that trials and adversity can be sanctifying and purifying, whether we are left on this earth or taken Home. God is with us, and we will come through all right if we can endure patiently. We need to develop increasing faith and trust in the wisdom of our Heavenly Father and His Holy Son, Jesus Christ.

Joseph Smith, experiencing one of his many "fiery furnaces" in Liberty Jail in March 1839, wrote the following to the Saints, who were also suffering:

> And now, beloved brethren, we say unto you, that inasmuch as God hath said that He would have a tried people, that He would purge them as gold, now we think that this time He has chosen His own crucible, wherein we have been tried; and we think if we get through with any degree of safety, and shall have kept the faith, that it will be a sign to this generation, altogether sufficient to leave them without excuse; and we think also, it will be a trial of our faith equal to that of Abraham, and that the ancients will not have whereof to boast over us in the day of judgment, as being called to pass through heavier afflictions. (*History of The Church of Jesus Christ of Latter-day Saints*, 7 vols. [Salt Lake City: The Church of Jesus Christ of Latter-day Saints, 1932–51), 3:294)

President Lorenzo Snow said more about the reality that we are to be proved in all things.

> Our trials and sufferings give us experience, and establish within us principles of godliness. The Lord will test the Saints. The Latter-day Saints have done wonders; but they cannot cease from doing wonders in the future. There will be greater things demanded of the Latter-day Saints than have ever been demanded since the organization of the Church. The Lord has determined in His heart that He will try us until He knows what He can do with us. He tried His Son Jesus. Thousands of years before He came upon earth,

the Father had watched His course and knew that He could depend upon Him when the salvation of worlds should be at stake; and He was not disappointed. So in regard to ourselves. He will try us, and continue to try us, in order that He may place us in the highest positions in life and put upon us the most sacred responsibilities. (*Journal of Discourses*, 26 vols. [London: Latter-day Saints' Book Depot, 1956–86], 26:368)

Even for the Savior, suffering was part of His education. "Who in the days of his flesh, when he had offered up prayers and supplications with strong crying and tears unto him that was able to save him from death, and was heard in that he feared;

"Though he were a Son, yet learned he obedience by the things which he suffered;

"And being made perfect, he became the author of eternal salvation unto all them that obey him" (Hebrews 5:7–9).

He was not just *a* son, but *the* Son! And yet He learned obedience through His suffering.

John Taylor said, "It is necessary men should be tried and purged and purified and made perfect through suffering" (*Journal of Discourses*, 20:305). We can also be made stronger. Henry Ward Beecher said that "affliction comes to us all—not to make us sad, but sober; not to make us sorry, but wise; not to make us despondent, but by its darkness to refresh us, as the night refreshes the day; not to impoverish, but to enrich us" (as quoted in *Church News*, 8 May 1989). He said it is a trial that will prove one thing weak and another strong, and that "a cobweb is as good as the mightiest cable when there is no strain upon it."

President Brigham Young taught that opposition and adversity give evidence that something *good* is happening. "God never bestows upon His people, or upon an individual, superior blessings without a severe trial to prove them, to prove that individual, or that people, to see whether they will keep their covenants with Him and keep in remembrance what He has shown them. Then the greater the vision, the greater the display of the power of the enemy" (*Journal of Discourses,* 3:205).

President Spencer W. Kimball also expressed the fact that truth stirs opposition:

> We are continually being tried and tested as individuals and as a church. There are more trials yet to come, but be not discouraged nor dismayed. Always remember that if this were not the Lord's work, the adversary would not pay any attention to us. If this Church were merely a church of men and women, teaching only the doctrines of men, we would encounter little or no criticism or resistance—but because this is the Church of him whose name it bears, we must not be surprised when criticisms or difficulties arise. With faith and good works, the truth will prevail. (*The Teachings of Spencer W. Kimball,* ed. Edward L. Kimball [Salt Lake City: Bookcraft, 1982], p. 182)

Elder James E. Faust said: "One of the advantages of having lived a long time is that you can often remember when you had it worse. I am grateful to have lived long enough to have known some of the blessings of adversity" (*Ensign,* May 1990, p. 85). Can we reach that point? Have you? Are you able to look back on your life with an increasing understanding of how important some of the "crash-and-burn" experiences have been in what matters to you most now?

One example comes from President Marion G. Romney, who experienced much adversity in his life and yet was such a cheerful, optimistic person. He said, "My soul has made its greatest growth as I have been driven to my knees by adversity and affliction" (Conference Report, October 1969, p. 60).

Our Heavenly Father, who knows us so completely, may need to do that to us from time to time: He may need to drive us to our knees to remind us of our relationship with Him and our complete dependence on Him for all that we have and all that we are.

I'm aware of feelings I have sometimes of wanting "quick cures," wanting to get rid of all the trials and tribulations that surround me and everyone. I've thought at times that if I were in charge, there may not be any hospitals or funerals.

President John Taylor, who was nearly killed in Carthage Jail with Joseph and Hyrum, offered some interesting insight on this point: "I used to think, if I were the Lord, I would not suffer people to be tried as they are. But I have changed my mind on that subject. Now I think I would, if I were the Lord, because it purges out the meanness and corruption that stick around the saints, like flies around molasses" (*Journal of Discourses*, 5:115).

Elder Orson F. Whitney wrote:

> No pain that we suffer, no trial that we experience is wasted. It ministers to our education, to the development of such qualities as patience, faith, fortitude and humility. All that we suffer and all that we endure, especially when we endure it patiently, builds up our characters, purifies our hearts, expands our souls, and makes us more tender and charitable, more worthy to be called the children of God. . . . And it is through sorrow and suffering, toil and tribulation, that we gain the education that we come here to acquire and which will make us more like our Father and Mother in heaven. (As quoted in Spencer W. Kimball, *Faith Precedes the Miracle* [Salt Lake City: Deseret Book, 1972], p. 98)

We can't avoid all adversity in our lives, but we certainly can do something about our response to it and our attitude toward it! President David O. McKay commented that "a martyr at the stake may have happiness that a king on his throne might envy" (Conference Report, October 1955, p. 8).

That reminds me of Victor Frankl's beautifully written, thought-provoking book, *Man's Search for Meaning*. He suffered terribly, including almost unbearable torture, in Nazi death camps. He survived and wrote, "Everything can be taken from a man but one thing: the last of the human freedoms—to choose one's attitude in any given set of circumstances, to choose one's own way" (New York: Simon and Schuster, 1973, p. 86). He realized at some point that he was actually more free than those who were guarding him. He found that he (and some others) could live in serenity and peace even in the most terrible conditions.

There must be effort on our part to face and deal with adversity. Discouragement must be replaced by encouragement. Courage is a great attribute to have when trials come.

Elder Neal A. Maxwell explained, "Jesus was of good cheer because then current conditions did not alter His sources of ultimate joy. Are not our fundamental sources of joy the same as His?" (*Even As I Am* [Salt Lake City: Deseret Book, 1982], p. 100). Take some time to ponder that thought: Our fundamental sources of joy are the same as the Savior's! What would you include? Prayer? Service? Obedience? Making the will of our Father *our* will? What were the Savior's fundamental sources of joy?

Do you know some who are pressing forward through their adversities with "a perfect brightness of hope"? (2 Nephi 31:20). I'd like to invite you to try an experiment of sorts. You may want to close your eyes to do this once you've read the explanation. In your mind (or literally, someday when you have the time), walk or ride around the area where you live and "look in" on neighbors and friends.

Remind yourself of some of the adversity that is evident in the lives of those whom you know and love, as well as in the lives of others whom you don't know as well. See if your journey takes you to a home (or apartment or dorm or condo or office) where there is someone going through an extremely difficult trial who is nevertheless happy and cheerful. Can you find someone in your mind's journey who is that way? Does that person teach you something about faith, and courage, and perspective?

I've always been inspired by the story of the Battle of Waterloo. An impending assault by the French army was reported to the Duke of Wellington, with the advice that his British troops be withdrawn. He replied, "Stand firm!" The soldiers obeyed, and the British won the Battle of Waterloo. When the Duke of Wellington was discussing this later, he said, "British soldiers are not braver than French soldiers, they are only brave five minutes longer" (as quoted in *Christ's Ideals for Living* [Salt Lake City: Deseret Sunday School Union Board, 1955]).

There are times when we have to "stand firm!" And with faith and courage, we can do that for "five minutes longer." I'm aware of the fact that there have been, are, and will continue to be countless examples of circumstances where individuals, families, and groups of people have been *happy* in the midst of *adversity*. They have had a healthy attitude!

I remember many of the stories shared during the sesquicentennial of the pioneers' arrival in the Salt Lake Valley. These pioneer stories tell of faithfulness and good cheer even in the midst of terrible suffering. Those faithful Saints didn't just spend day after day gritting their teeth and wondering "how long." Rather, they sang and danced with their wagons pulled into great circles for the night. Those who survived lived lives of gratitude and service rather than letting some bitterness or anger ruin their peace and their souls.

There's a difference between just "going through" something and what we call "enduring." Elder Marvin J. Ashton helped point out the difference to me in one of his talks in general conference: "Greatness is best measured by how well an individual responds to the happenings in life that appear to be totally unfair, unreasonable, and undeserved. Sometimes we are inclined to put up with a situation rather than endure. To endure is to bear up under, to stand firm against, to suffer

91

without yielding, to continue to be, or to exhibit the state or power of lasting" (*Ensign*, November 1984, p. 22).

Elder Neal A. Maxwell reminds us that "True enduring represents not merely the passage of time, but the passage of the soul—and not merely from A to B, but sometimes all the way from A to Z. To endure in faith and do God's will (see D&C 63:20; 101:35) therefore involves much more than putting up with difficult circumstances" (*Ensign*, May 1990, p. 34).

I have wondered about the "enduring" part of life. We lived for so many millions of years with our Heavenly Father. Surely He already knows us very well. Why does He have to "prove" our capacity to endure? Elder Maxwell explains this one to me so well: "But does not God know beforehand if we can endure? Yes, perfectly. But we need to know, firsthand, about our capacity. So much of a life well lived consists of coming to know what God knows already" (*Wherefore, Ye Must Press Forward* [Salt Lake City: Deseret Book, 1977], p. 110).

Elder Marvin J. Ashton reminded us that "Enduring, or carrying on, is not just a matter of tolerating circumstances and hanging in there, but of pressing forward. I know that's what most of us find difficult—to endure joyfully" (*Ensign*, November 1989, p. 36).

God can and does help that happen. As we learn to trust our Heavenly Father and the Savior, we are more likely to notice all the ways in which we are comforted, blessed, and lifted. We may be more able to turn ourselves and our lives over to Them, knowing that *They know what They're doing*, and They want us to be happy and return to live with Them.

Read again the wonderful way President Ezra Taft Benson has taught about this: "Men and women who turn their lives over to God will discover that He can make a lot more out of their lives than they can. He will deepen their joys, expand their vision, quicken their minds, strengthen their muscles, lift their spirits, multiply their blessings, increase their opportunities, comfort their souls, raise up friends, and pour out peace. Whoever will lose his life in the service of God will find eternal life (see Matthew 10:39)" (*The Teachings of Ezra Taft Benson* [Salt Lake City: Bookcraft, 1988], p. 361).

Read through his comments at least two or three times. See if you can remember some help you've received that you hadn't realized, or which you hadn't thought about for quite some time, or for which you haven't yet been thankful. Also see if you can find some blessings you need right now, and then work to turn your life over to the One who really does know what He's doing, and who will do all He can to help you find happiness amidst your trials.

This is the way, then: not to avoid trials and adversity, not to be immune from the many challenges that come to *all* of Heavenly Father's children, but to *endure*, to hold on to hope and faith. As Alma counseled his son Helaman: "I beseech of thee that thou wilt hear my words and learn of me; for I do know that whosoever shall put their trust in God shall be supported in their trials, and their troubles, and their afflictions, and shall be lifted up at the last day" (Alma 36:3).

The message given to Joseph Smith in the Doctrine and Covenants is a message for us too: "Be patient in afflictions, for thou shalt have many; but endure them, for, lo, I am with thee, even unto the end of thy days" (D&C 24:8).

The Savior was with Joseph, and He will be with us. He experienced enough (and more) in Gethsemane to understand anything and everything that we might feel. *Anything!* There is no sorrow, no anguish, no suffering beyond His ability to understand—to feel with us—and to comfort and visit.

Like you, I often turn to the hymns for comfort and consolation. I think you will find sweet comfort in these beautiful words.

> *Come, ye disconsolate, where'er ye languish;*
> *Come to the mercy seat, fervently kneel.*

Here bring your wounded hearts; here tell your anguish.
Earth has no sorrow that heav'n cannot heal.

Joy of the desolate, Light of the straying,
Hope of the penitent, fadeless and pure!
Here speaks the Comforter, tenderly saying,
"Earth has no sorrow that heav'n cannot cure."

Here see the Bread of Life; see waters flowing
Forth from the throne of God, pure from above.
Come to the feast of love; come, ever knowing
Earth has no sorrow but heav'n can remove.
(Hymns, no. 115)

Oh, I *know* this is true. These words bring tears to my eyes. There is no sorrow that heaven cannot heal, cure, and remove! Please know that. Please *feel that* as you go through your deep water and fiery trials. *Know* that you're not alone. Bring your wounded hearts. Tell your anguish. Listen to the Comforter—let Him do His job. Come to the mercy seat. Come to the feast of love!

"And God shall wipe away all tears from their eyes; and there shall be no more death, neither sorrow, nor crying, neither shall there be any more pain: for the former things are passed away" (Revelation 21:4).

I am convinced deep in my soul that Jesus has more than enough power and love and experience to understand, succor, comfort, sanctify, rescue, heal, bless, and save. He knows what we feel and why. He has more than enough power and love and experience to be our Brother, our Everlasting Friend, our Savior, King, Redeemer, Prince of Peace, and Good Shepherd. He's knocking. Let Him in.

Chapter 6

WENDELL'S TRIUMPH OVER ADVERSITY

WHEN I THINK OF HAPPINESS IN adversity, one man always comes to my mind. He wrote to me once about happiness, trying to describe some of what he was feeling at a particular high and joyful point in his life.

But I'm getting ahead of myself. I need to go back a few years, to the summer of 1964. I was just finishing a two-year mission adventure in Southeast Asia, but life in Mapleton, Utah, was going on pretty much as usual that summer.

I remember hearing about the accident. Wendell was sixteen years old. It was a hot day, and he'd been working in the hay with his friends. Have you ever worked in the fields? If you have, you probably know something about how much this group of friends looked forward to the end of their workday when it was time to swim!

Toward late afternoon, they went to the pond in the southeast part of Mapleton, a place where they'd often go to cool off after a hard day of work. They were jumping and diving and generally enjoying themselves. Suddenly, on one dive, Wendell hit a shallow place where the sand and dirt had shifted. In an instant his neck was broken.

At first his friends thought he was clowning around,

trying to tease them by staying under the water. He almost drowned before they realized he was in serious trouble and rescued him.

I remember hearing about some people's comments: "They should have let him die. What kind of a future does he have? He'll never experience any kind of normal life as a quadriplegic. He'd have been better off if they had let him die."

But he didn't die. And the world and a whole lot of us in it are better off because he didn't. We have been blessed because of his extraordinary life.

Wendell Bird Johnson was born on March 26, 1948, to Orpha Dee and Frank Johnson of Mapleton, Utah. He was a creative, healthy, happy little boy. He had many friends and many interests.

One friend, Tom Nielsen, told of the first time the two of them met. It was the summer before they were to start kindergarten, and Tom was so excited that a boy his age had moved in on Main Street.

He said that at that first meeting, Wendell was wearing his Red Ryder cowboy outfit: chaps, hat, vest, and two cap guns, one on each hip. And so began the adventure of their friendship.

One afternoon, Wendell had built a parachute out of an old sheet and a wicker fishing creel. He explained to Tom that he was going to climb to the top of the giant swing set his dad had built in the backyard and would use the huge four-seat glider as the jump-off point to try out the parachute.

With a lot of huffing and puffing, the two of them got the glider swinging to the full height of the swing set, and then, with a yell of terror, Wendell made the leap. The fishing creel opened, and the parachute deployed perfectly at about the exact instant Wendell hit the ground. The parachute floated down and covered him. He didn't move.

Tom hurried to get the glider stopped, and then went over

and pulled the chute off Wendell, who rolled over, managed a bit of a smile, and said, "I'm never going to do that again!"

There were normal, happy childhood adventures, including football in the park, chasing fish at Utah Lake, movies, Scouting, and many hours talking about girls and cars and other interests. Wendell had a love of music and learned to play the banjo, but his main interest remained art. Teachers at school were always trying to keep Wendell's attention on his studies and lessons, but he was always drawing.

Wendell showed a natural ability for drawing at a very early age. "My favorite pastime was to go to the Springville Museum of Art during my free time to study the paintings," he said. He decided that a career in some branch of the arts was the only life for him, and hoped to someday become an architect.

And then the accident happened. Almost everything changed suddenly and dramatically. This was a time of tremendous adjustment, particularly for Wendell and his parents.

There were long periods of hospitalization at first. I remember going to visit Wendell at the University of Utah Hospital when I returned from my mission. He made friends with everyone, including patients and staff members who came to love and enjoy him very much.

Finally he was able to go home. His parents had moved a hospital bed into a sunny room with lots of windows in the back of the house, and that would become "headquarters" for Wendell for the next eleven years.

Everyone in the family became involved in helping and caring for their son and brother. His sister Brenda remembers that Wendell always stuck up for all of them. He was a peacemaker. He didn't like arguing or fighting.

He also had an unusually wonderful sense of humor. His younger brother Paul tells of helping their father pour cement to make the front porch on their home. Wendell was sitting outside in his wheelchair watching. While mixing the cement,

Paul accidentally raised up into a tree branch so hard that it knocked him over.

He said that when he stood up, he glanced over to see that Wendell was dangling out of his wheelchair! He quickly ran over to see what was wrong, only to realize that Wendell had slipped out because he was laughing so hard!

Morris, the youngest brother, was sixteen when Wendell was called as the priests quorum advisor. Morris remembers watching him read and then ponder, trying to get the lesson just right for the young men who would come to his home during priesthood meeting. "He didn't like us to goof around," says Morris. "He wanted to teach us something."

Morris also remembers how many friends used to come and visit Wendell in their home after the accident. He said he loved sticking around with his big brother, watching the people come and go and listening to the conversations.

I was one of those visitors, along with my younger sister Susan. We really enjoyed our visits with Wendell, but I soon noticed that she was going more often alone than with me. Morris noticed it too, especially when one day Susan and Wendell said to him, "Haven't you got someplace to go, Morris?" That was when he and the rest of us began to realize that the friendship had grown to something deeper and sweeter.

It was several years before the two were married. Wendell told her that he loved her too much to ask her to take care of him for the rest of his life. He did *not* want pity. And that's certainly not what she was offering.

When Wendell told Susan he was certain she could marry anyone she wanted, she announced that she guessed she would never marry, because the one she *wanted* to marry wouldn't ask her. "If I can't marry the man I love, I just won't get married, period," she said stubbornly.

So he asked.

Elder Neal A. Maxwell has said that "the everlastingness of certain things puts the temporariness of other things in perspective" (*Even As I Am* [Salt Lake City: Deseret Book, 1982], p. 98). This seems to have been especially true and on everyone's mind on that beautiful August day when Wendell and Susan were married in the Provo Temple. Those of us who were there will never forget that holy, extraordinary day.

Susan reported that when she married Wendell, several people had said things like, "Oh, you're so wonderful to have married that Johnson boy." Then, when they got to know him better, they'd say to her, "You're so fortunate!" She always felt fortunate and blessed.

Not many days after they were married, I was visiting one day and Wendell asked, quite seriously, "Melon, how long do you think it's appropriate for the bride to carry the groom over the threshold? It's been quite a few days now, and she keeps doing it!"

Immediately following the accident, Wendell had spent some time at a rehabilitation center in California. While there, he worked extremely hard to gain a limited amount of use of his shoulders and biceps.

A special hand brace was made to enable him to hold a pencil. Because of his very limited movement, he had to learn to write and draw and paint all over again. He described it as trying to write upside down and sideways.

"At first it was frustrating—like beginning all over again as a child," he said. "I was only able to scribble." But with persistence and determination, Wendell continued to work until he was doing thumbnail sketches. Two years later he graduated from pencil to brush and watercolor. In 1968, Wendell began painting in oils.

This hand brace also enabled Wendell to hold other tools, such as one he used for pushing buttons on the phone and for typing. But don't imagine typing as you've ever known it. I've watched him type many times, and I'm not sure how to describe how long it would take, letter by letter. I wonder what his timed speed would be—maybe one or two words per minute, *if* they were short words.

Once I wanted to feel more empathy for this slow, laborious process. The only thing I could think of was to hold a pencil between my two smallest toes and try to type. I kept wanting to use my hands to straighten out the pencil or hold it still. Even at that, I really couldn't come very close to knowing what it was like for Wendell. But he did a *lot* of writing, including scripts and directors' notes for several short films.

Once he wrote about the way people would sometimes approach him only as a handicapped person. He said it was hard to remain patient when people would approach him speaking loudly, as if he couldn't hear them, or when they'd think his brain had been damaged and they'd talk to him in short, choppy sentences rather than just conversing normally.

When he was in the hospital some would say things like, "Now remember, don't chase the nurses down the hall!" or, "Be a good boy and take your medicine!" or, "How do you like that awful-lookin' food?"

Then there were those who asked things like, "Would you like me to get in touch with the missionaries? Why, just a week ago they—oh, they're so wonderful—they healed my big toe! Oh! I just know they could fix you up!"

And then Wendell wrote, "Is *this* what I was spared for? To answer people's questions and listen to their stupid comments? They seem to think this is what I want to talk about, or that this is the extent of conversation I'm able to talk about. They avoid their real thoughts, which are thoughts of ignorance and pity."

He went on, "I must admit that there are, fortunately, very few such people. Most are very kind and understanding. But they avoid the handicapped as much as possible. This is their secret—to act as if they understand, but, inside, they can't stand the sight of atrophied, wasted limbs." He said they would hide behind excuses: "I just don't know what to say to him." "I feel so sorry for him." "I can't seem to think of anything to say to sympathize with him."

Wendell's parents endured some of the same kind of responses from people: "He was such a promising boy." "Maybe he has a mission in life, but if he doesn't, I just know that in the Millennium he'll be healed."

Wendell wrote that the question he got that seemed to top them all went something like this: "Why don't you get out and associate more? People are so interesting. You may even enjoy yourself." People *were* interesting, and Wendell *did* enjoy them. Some never quite realized what they had missed when they categorized him and quit coming to visit.

Others found in Wendell one of the most erudite, interesting, and wonderful individuals they had ever met. His accomplishments were many and varied. He held many Church callings and often spoke at special firesides. He served as justice of the peace for six years, and then as Mapleton's mayor from 1982 to 1986.

Wendell worked from his bed with a desk attachment designed and built by his father. Susan would get everything set up, depending on what he wanted to work on, and then, with infinite patience and persistence, he'd carefully go about his work. A painting would often take from eight months to a year to complete because of his love of making each one full of detail and beauty. "When I paint, I forget about being handicapped," he said. "I am pulled into the dimensions of the canvas before me, and I feel free."

My favorite of Wendell's paintings is the one he did for me. He had wanted to do an oil painting for me, and after a few years of thinking about it, I asked him if he would do one of the Savior based on a calendar picture I had seen in the sixties. He worked on it for many months before inviting me over for the "unveiling."

When I look at my picture of the Savior, which appears on the back cover of this book, I know that Wendell is well acquainted with Jesus, and I feel more deeply about the cost of the Atonement for me personally. I know that Jesus was the only one who could say to Wendell, "I know just how you feel," without Wendell thinking inside, "No, you don't—you have *no idea.*" Jesus *did* and *does.* And He knows that for *all* and for *each* of us!

It's almost as if, when I look at this painting, I can imagine the Savior as my Advocate with the Father, saying "Let her in—she meant well." In the painting I see such compassion and tenderness along with such strength and power.

Would Wendell have been better off if they had let him die? Or was his life a glorious opportunity for the Lord to manifest His miracles?

One of the miracles that Susan and Wendell experienced was the birth of their daughter.

I was in Indonesia when Wendy Sue was born on January 1, 1977. In some ways I'm glad I was a long ways away, because Wendell wrote me a long letter to describe all that happened. Having watched him type many times, I know it took him a *long* time to type it. It is one of my treasures, a sort of "treatise on happiness." The following excerpts will show you what I mean:

> Mapleton, Utah
> January 20, 1977
> Magnificent Melon
> Bamboo Acres, Where Am I? Road
> Hungawa, Indonesia
> Dearest Melon, Jungle Woman, Queen Kong,
> Wendy Sue Johnson IS!!! As you probably are aware she was born at 8:36 A.M. on Jan. 1, 1977. What a bright, alert little spirit she is. Enclosed is your very own copy of her

day 1 photograph. I would have written sooner but we wanted to send you visual proof of her existence.

Already her little personality asserts itself. She has strong lungs and really cries up a storm whenever she is hungry or has a dirty diaper. She loves to look around at the light and space around her with her big dark green eyes. In calmer moments she makes a variety of little coos and gurgling noises, and has mastered a little grunting sound that is very much like that of a baby bear cub.

He goes on to describe her physical appearance in the usual proud-father terms, and then he writes:

There have been many times in my life that I have known happiness, but it seems now that the joys of the past are insignificant compared to the unspeakable happiness of the present. Even the term *happiness* has assumed a different meaning. I know that people seek after it in many different forms and many varied manifestations—both true and false. I know that some have found it in self-abnegation, self-sacrifice, serving one's fellow men, devoting one's life to a cause, losing one's self in work, achieving a sense of security, accumulating material wealth or possession, etc., etc. But in this life there are degrees of happiness that transcend anything that I have ever experienced before.

I found happiness in purpose, achievement of goals, and striving to progress on a positive plane toward an ideal, but ultimately I found it in this miraculous act of creation. It seems solemnly appropriate that new life should emerge as the product of love—as its highest purpose and achievement.

Is happiness possible in the midst of adversity? Wendell's life testified every day that it is.

Right from the moment Wendy Sue was born, there was something extremely special in her relationship with her daddy. She'd sit for hours with him in his bed, learning how to mix paint and make all the colors of the rainbow. He was always there for her—literally.

Wendell's dad helped make a little battery-powered car for him—a comfortable chair on a platform with wheels. Many times I'd see him, with Wendy on his lap, headed toward the foothills and canyons, or on his way to visit his parents, a few blocks from home. More than a few times the batteries went dead before he made it back, and we'd go out hunting for him and "plug him in" so he could make it back to home base.

I remember a time several years ago when his birthday was approaching and I asked Wendy if she had a gift for him. She seemed sobered by the question and said she had told him what she wanted to give him and he had refused. I asked what it was. She said she told him she'd like to trade him places for just one day—she wanted to give him the chance to get up and go places, to drive a car, to run and jump and go wherever he wanted.

I asked her what her dad had said, and she got choked up. He told her he wouldn't want her or anyone to trade places with him for even an hour. He wouldn't wish that on *anyone*, and he certainly wouldn't allow Wendy to go through what he was going through if he could help it.

Actually, it's small wonder that Wendy had such empathy for her dad. She is so much like him that some of us call her the "Wendell clone." She particularly has his eyes, his gentleness, and his talent for art. As of the writing of this book, Wendy is twenty-two years old and is finishing a degree in fine arts with an oil painting emphasis at Brigham Young University. She's also been involved in computer animation. A lot of Wendell carries on in this world through her.

On Sunday, March 17, 1996, I visited Wendell in the intensive care unit of the hospital. It certainly wasn't his first hospital visit, but we had a sense that he might be going home in a different direction this time. Here are some things I wrote in my journal that night:

No one was with him. He seemed glad to see me. I gave him a hug and a kiss. I sat by his side and had a most interesting feeling of peace and calm. It's difficult for me to explain. I felt very close to Wendell even though we didn't talk a whole lot. Tears kept coming. He'd close his eyes and I'd cry and think and pray. . . .

For quite a while I had a very strong impression that there were angels in the room. I didn't see anything, but I *felt*. Strongly. I talked to them quietly. "Are you getting ready to come and take Wendell Home? Is the time getting close?"

The whole time I was with him was very spiritual and sweet.

The following day, Monday, my brother Frank and I visited Wendell in the evening. We didn't know it would be our last time to visit him—and yet we did, somehow. We stayed for about an hour and had such a good time. We laughed a lot, but our feelings were very tender. I kept feeling like I wanted to cry. We left very slowly and reluctantly that night. I found myself asking Heavenly Father if and when Wendell might be able to come Home. Had he—and we—learned enough by then?

I drove slowly. I felt like I wasn't part of the going-home traffic. I was somewhere else. I was away from it, removed from it, thinking and feeling so much so deeply.

Early the next morning, Tuesday, March 19, 1996, Frank called me from the hospital. He started to say something and then couldn't. The tears came. He said, "Here, I'll let Susan talk to you." And then I knew. Susan confirmed it when she came on the line: "I just wanted to let you know that he's gone."

The nurses had called her at 4:00 A.M. Wendell had been having a hard time breathing, and the staff wanted to know again Susan's feelings (and Wendell's) about heroics should he need some help. Susan assured them they didn't want any extraordinary measures taken to delay what was going to happen. They were ready. It was time for Wendell to go Home.

Once the staff was sure that this was what Susan and Wendell had decided, they unhooked all the equipment except for some monitors. And they left the two of them alone.

Susan said Wendell wasn't able to talk to her at that point, but still they communicated tenderly during the next half hour while they waited for the time to come when he would be taken Home.

Susan said he would look at her and then over into the corner. She said she knew there were loved ones, angels, who were there waiting. She could sense that. She would have liked to ask him who it was, but she realized he didn't have any extra energy to talk to her. But, again, with his eyes he communicated as she talked to him quietly.

Susan sensed that Wendell wanted to make sure again that it would be all right with Wendy Sue if he should leave. Sue had a cell phone with her; she called Wendy and put the phone to Wendell's ear. Wendy told her dad how much she loved him, but that it was all right for him to go, that she and Susan would be all right.

After Wendy hung up, Susan told him the same thing again: "Wendell, when they come this time you've *got* to go with them." It was time to quit fighting and struggling and suffering. Everyone here would be all right and would take care of each other.

I think it was important for them to spend this final half hour together, just the two of them, knowing it wouldn't be long before they'd say good-bye for a little while. I can't think of this sacred, holy time without remembering a description in Doctrine and Covenants 88:95: "And there shall be silence in heaven for the space of half an hour; and immediately after shall the curtain of heaven be unfolded, as a scroll is unfolded after it is rolled up, and the face of the Lord shall be unveiled."

And, truly, the veil was taken away and Wendell was able to once again see the Savior's face.

> Now, concerning the state of the soul between death and the resurrection—Behold, it has been made known unto me by an angel, that the spirits of all men, as soon as they are departed from this mortal body, yea, the spirits of all men, whether they be good or evil, are taken home to that God who gave them life.
>
> And then shall it come to pass, that the spirits of those who are righteous are received into a state of happiness, which is called paradise, a state of rest, a state of peace, where they shall rest from all their troubles and from all care, and sorrow. (Alma 40:11–12)

At Wendell's funeral service a few days later, my brother Frank shared these thoughts:

> When an accident happens with a tragic result, as in Wendell's young life, a lot of times you wonder why—why did this happen to me? Why do I have to go through this adversity? Too often the obsession with "why" leads to bitterness and self-pity.
>
> In the years I've known Wendell and in the hours and the days I've spent with him, never have I heard Wendell ever question "Why me?" And I've never seen an ounce of self-pity. His life of patience and caring about others replaced any would-be bitterness with a sweet life, and self-pity with accomplishments. . . .
>
> I see several parables, changed just a little bit, that apply to Wendell's life. I see a bushel exploding with the light of the bright noonday sun. I see Wendell being given one talent and returning fifty. I see a little bewildered and confused mustard seed springing forth as a great Sequoia.

Did Wendell's life have purpose? Did he experience happiness? Can you see how everything—everything!—is part of that great plan of happiness?

President Spencer W. Kimball put some of my feelings into words when he talked of those who have become angels through their trials:

> Have you ever seen someone who has been helpless for so long that he has divested himself of every envy and jealousy and ugliness in his whole life, and who has perfected his life? . . . No pain suffered by man or woman upon the earth will be without its compensating effects if it be suffered in resignation and if it be met with patience. . . . I'm grateful that my priesthood power is limited and used as the Lord sees fit to use it. . . . Sickness sometimes is a great blessing. People become angels through sickness. (*The Teachings of Spencer W. Kimball* [Salt Lake City: Bookcraft, 1982], pp. 167–68.)

Has this been your experience? It surely has been mine through my close association with an angel named Wendell Johnson. I'm grateful for his willingness to endure to the end in his mortal body, that we might learn and grow from his example. I look forward to meeting him in that day when his "soul shall be restored to the body, and the body to the soul; yea, and every limb and joint shall be restored to its body; yea, even a hair of the head shall not be lost; but all things shall be restored to their proper and perfect frame" (Alma 40:23).

Chapter 7

GRATITUDE: THE HAPPY ATTITUDE!

I DON'T REMEMBER WHERE I WAS when I was struck by the notion of "relativity." It certainly wasn't that I suddenly understood what Einstein had been trying to tell the world. I don't even know enough about his theory to know if it would have any connection at all to my own simple version.

Let me see if I can introduce my own personal "Theory of Relativity" with a little story I found at least thirty years ago (and have long since forgotten where I found it):

Two little children were put early to bed on a winter's night, for the fire had gone out, and the cold was pouring in at the many cracks of their frail shanty. The mother strove to eke out the scantiness of the bedcovering by placing clean boards over the children. A pair of bright eyes shone out from under a board, and just before it was hushed in slumber, a sweet voice said, "Mother, how nice this is! How I pity the poor people who don't have any boards to cover their children with this cold night."

This story touches me deeply. Here is a little girl who is *grateful*. She's not like me—comparing what she has with the possessions of those who have so much more. Quite the opposite: She is not only thankful for what she has but concerned

109

about those who (relatively speaking) have less than she does—those who don't have clean boards on a cold night.

I've thought a lot about this little girl. Surely she'd heard about or even seen things like an electric blanket or a heating pad or even warmed-up bricks. Likely she knew that others had so much more than she did—so many elaborate, expensive ways of getting and keeping warm. Yet she was grateful for what she had. She was thankful for her *present blessings*. Her appreciation was based on her perspective of what she did have, not what she didn't have.

Why am I not more that way? I picture myself in that little girl's place and can imagine myself complaining, "Mommy, I'm going to get slivers!" Or checking to see if in fact my sister Charlotte's boards were bigger and better than mine.

Do you do that too, sometimes? Do you find yourself skipping over gratitude for what you have because you know there's someone who has more? It's not hard to do. Maybe you've seen the picture of four cows in adjoining pastures, each with its head over the fence, eating the "greener grass" in the pasture next to its own.

The "Theory of Relativity" recognizes that there will always be many who have more and fancier stuff than ours. We could make ourselves miserable for the rest of our lives by focusing on this fact, continually comparing and complaining and feeling unsatisfied, unthankful, uncontent. It disturbs my peace when I get caught in such an unending loop of comparison based on "things" and "stuff."

I remember when Ann Laemmlen and I were sent to live in Nigeria, West Africa, to help with a child health project. We lived in a village called Eket, in the Cross River State. The closest "big cities" were Calabar, Aba, and Port Harcourt.

The building where we were to live was a large one because we were anticipating more team members as the project grew, and it was to be our office as well as our home. It had wires for electricity, but there was none in the community except where there were generators. On a very few occasions while we were there, we would have power for maybe an hour or two at a time. There were pipes, but we rarely had water, and when we did we saved it in every possible container, only to watch the thick, scary stuff accumulate on the surface. (Ann would write me notes in the scum.)

There was no bed, table, chair, desk, cupboard, or shelf. There was just the big, empty place. And so, with some sarcasm in our voices, we called it The Palace. We would joke about it being on the cover of *Better Homes and Gardens*. Ha.

Couple missionaries living in small apartments next to The Palace were kind enough to let us stay with them while we went through the process of preparing the place. Meanwhile we began to meet our neighbors—those who would be participating in the child health project, and members of our branch, and other people in the community. As we went to their homes and saw how they lived, we began to understand more about life in Eket.

Gradually, we came to realize that The Palace really *was* a palace! We had a floor. We had screens on the windows. We had water sometimes and electricity occasionally, and we were getting beds and chairs, tables and shelves, cupboards and a stove.

Children loved coming to The Palace and running their bare feet along the smooth floor. One day a pipe that came out from a wall in the bathroom—which pipe was high enough on the wall to be a shower if and when we ever got some water—began to drip. The kids acted like they were seeing a miracle! They ran and put their faces under the drips, taking turns, getting back in line to have another turn. They apparently had never seen anything like it. Indoor water!

Our big, empty, wonderful place truly became The Palace to

us, and thanks to relativity we became grateful—extremely grateful—for such a beautiful place in which to live.

I've had so many important teachers who have helped me learn and deeply understand this "Theory of Relativity." Many of them live in other places, like Asia and Africa. One of the most powerful of these teachers is Sukiman (pronounced Soo-kee-mawn).

Sukiman and several other Church members lived in a Chinese cemetery near the beautiful city of Surakarta in Central Java, Indonesia. Their place was called Jebres, and they were always inviting me and my companion to come and visit them.

One day we did just that—we rode our bikes on the dirt road for some distance until we came to Jebres and the little village in the Chinese cemetery. The members were so happy to see us. They showed us where to put our bikes, and then we followed them down a jungle-like trail into the village, into the cemetery.

We had the privilege of visiting in several homes. One belonged to a dear soul named Ibu Juariah. ("Ibu" is a title, like "Mrs." or "Mother." Indonesians don't have a "first" and "last" name—they just have a name, like Sukiman.)

Ibu Juariah had a small home made mostly of bamboo. On one wall she had a poster of Donny Osmond, purple socks and all. I'm sure I asked her where she got that poster, but I can't remember now what she said. She had found out, though, that Donny Osmond was a Mormon, and she was thrilled to have his picture on her wall.

The last home we visited was Sukiman's place. He, like the others, had built his little home out of whatever he could find—mostly bamboo. He'd made a bench so that my companion and I could sit down while we visited. He and his wife and the others who had followed us through the little village sat on the dirt floor. And we began to talk.

I asked Sukiman a question that I thought was rather run-of-the-mill: "How many children do you have?" Something unspoken passed between him and his wife, and then he responded. "Suster, tidak ada keturunan"—*there is no one following us.* It wasn't just "We don't have any children." In the Indonesian language it was more like "There is no posterity—there is no one to follow us."

Then he added, as if in explanation, "We have had children, but we didn't know how to care for them, and they all died." That hurt. It didn't seem fair—not when so many of us knew so much about caring for children and had so many resources to help us. I thought of myself and how pleasant my childhood had been, with enough and to spare of everything I needed and wanted.

We kept talking. At one point Sukiman asked, "Sister, do the members of the Church in other parts of the world pray for me?" In the next nanosecond I sure had a lot go through my mind. I realized I hadn't even known where Indonesia *was*, let alone prayed for anyone who might live there.

Yet I knew that there were and are leaders and members who know that Heavenly Father's children *all* need His blessings, and so I could honestly answer the question: "Yes, Sukiman, there are many members of the Church in other parts of the world who pray for you." He became emotional and said sincerely, "Bagus, Suster! Isn't that *wonderful?* I pray for them, too."

Sukiman prays for us. He in his small bamboo home prays for us in our split-level comfort.

This was in 1977, and we were receiving letters from home about the shortage of water in Utah and the surrounding area. It was a year when there wasn't enough snow and rain, and everyone was concerned.

The Indonesian members would ask us, "What do you hear from your family? What do you hear from home?" And so we told them about the water shortage, and they became worried even though they couldn't imagine what snow was, or irrigation, or sprinklers.

Things became "relative" in a powerful way one day when one missionary's mother sent him a clipping from a newspaper in California. It reported that in a part of California the people were being restricted in their water usage—they had to cut down to only 120 gallons of water per household per day for everything they needed. Inside and out! *120 gallons!*

Imagining myself in that situation, I could almost hear myself complaining. "What? You can't do this to me! I can't make it on only 120 gallons a day! Do you realize how often I like to shower and wash my hair? Do you have any idea how many flowers I need to water? And what about my garden? Do you want me to *suffer?* Somebody's got to *do* something here!"

I could hear myself whining and complaining about this terrible sacrifice, this unbelievable curtailment in my use of water, this exceedingly annoying inconvenience. This disaster!

And then the "Theory of Relativity" kicked in once more. I thought of Sukiman. I found myself wondering, "What would Sukiman do with 120 gallons of water in one day?" I had to try to imagine if he could haul that much in his leaky bucket. It held less than a gallon, so it would take more than 120 round-trips to where he had to go to fetch water. Even if he worked for twenty-four hours, I realized, he would never be able to collect 120 gallons of water. Even if he could gather that much, he had nowhere to store it.

And then, most importantly perhaps, I thought about how the water in California was safe water—no beasties or germs to make someone sick. Sukiman's water was often a source of sickness; the only way he had of making it safe was to boil it, and there wasn't always enough fuel or time to do that.

And then it hit me "big time," right in my heart: 120 gallons of water is a whole lot of water. Relatively speaking, it's a *huge* amount of water. Ask anyone who's ever been on a hike with only a one-quart canteen. Ask anyone who's ever been in a situation where the water has gone off for an extended length of time—ask them what it would mean to have 120 gallons of water stored, ready for use. Ask anyone who lives in a place where water has to be gathered from a river or stream, day after day, and carried back to the home. Ask anyone who has almost *never* had the luxury of drinking all the water they wanted whenever they felt thirsty. Yes, 120 gallons is a *lot* of water.

During that month of February in 1977, we got a message from our mission president in Jakarta informing us that all the members of the Church throughout the world were going to fast and pray together on a particular Sunday. Everyone would pray for each other, for all the problems and challenges in the world that people were facing. Some had too much water and some didn't have enough. Some were troubled by earthquakes or typhoons, disease or loneliness. It was our understanding that we would unite our faith and our prayers for each other on this particular Sabbath.

We were to let the Indonesian members know about this special fast. This was an interesting feeling, because we were aware that many of them ate only one meal a day anyway, and not because they were fasting. But they responded, and I know they came to this particular meeting with the spirit of fasting and prayer.

As we gathered in our branch, one of the brothers was asked to pray, and I'll never forget the feeling I had. At one point I even opened my eyes, so deeply touched and impressed I was with what he was saying. "Heavenly Father, we understand that some of our brothers and sisters are suffering because they don't have enough water. We have *plenty*. Could You take some of our water and share it with them?"

Oh, my. It wouldn't surprise me at all to learn one day that in the spring of 1977, Heavenly Father allowed Sukiman and the others to share their water with their brothers and sisters in places they would never even be able to imagine, let alone visit.

I tried to grasp what I had learned from this experience. Much of it had to do with my narrowness and selfishness. Everything had revolved around me and my needs and wants so much of the time, for so much of my life. It struck me that if Sukiman was praying for me—for us—there might be others doing the same thing. Maybe someone in Bolivia, Australia, Denmark, or Brooklyn.

Do *we* pray for *them?* Sometimes I do. Sometimes I've accidentally watched the news and have been caught off guard by the report of some of Heavenly Father's children suffering—going through unbelievably cruel hardships—and I pray for them, my brothers and sisters. But I could do so more often, not just when prompted or pushed by the reality I see or hear or read about. Certainly there are always some of our Father's children who are hungry, thirsty, naked, sick, or imprisoned.

President Spencer W. Kimball challenged us to learn to view our own *wants* in light of others' *needs*. That is a powerful way for me to be increasingly honest and realistic about my wants and needs. Relatively speaking, I have few needs, and many of my wants are things I could get along without if I'd learn to be more grateful for what I already have (and may not use well or at all).

It has been my observation—mostly in observing myself, but also in watching others—that when I focus on what I *don't have*, I tend to become increasingly self-centered, selfish, and crabby. This is an easy trap to fall into, as there are and will always be many who have lots more than I do. I think there are reasons I'm still discovering why one of the Ten Commandments is "Thou shalt not covet." There is something sad and unnecessary about a life consumed by the obsession with getting more and better stuff.

We live in a culture where it's sometimes hard to be content and satisfied, to have *enough*. There will constantly be new, dazzling things, and new efforts to make us feel discontent (so that we'll want more of those things). There will always be a newer watch, a more powerful computer, a fancier cell phone, a car with more bells and whistles.

But *you can never get enough of what you don't need*, because what you don't need *never satisfies*. For me that's a life-changing thought. I can have a house or basement or storage unit filled with stuff and things, but if it's not what I *need*, it will never satisfy me, no matter how much I have.

We spend money we don't have to buy things we don't need to impress people we don't like . . . and then they don't come over! We're paying bills for these things we didn't really need, and no one's over here getting jealous! What happened?

President Ezra Taft Benson used to quote a little rhyme: "There, there, little luxury, don't you cry—you'll be a necessity by and by!" I like it. It reminds me of times when I have dreamed about, worked for, saved, and planned for something wonderful that was going to *satisfy* me. This thing was going to be a luxury for which I would be thankful the rest of my life. Many of those things that were going to be such luxuries became necessities right away.

I've talked to friends about this, and we've smiled about many specific things that have fallen in this category, from computers to microwaves, from cell phones to indoor plumbing.

Once when I was thinking seriously and deeply about all of this, I decided to make a list of luxuries. I began writing down items with a number "2" in front of each, saying to myself that one of something was needed, but two would be luxury. And at the top of the list I wrote "2 homes." Absolutely—one home is needed, but two is luxury.

I think this particular item—a home—came to mind because of the memory of being in sacrament meeting as a little girl and hearing someone say, as they closed a meeting with prayer, "Take us to our various homes in safety." I was amazed! *Various* homes? How many did they have? I could sort of picture the family meeting in the foyer after the meeting and the father asking, "Which home shall we go to?" and one of the children responding, "Oh, Dad, let's go to number 3— it's got the best food!"

Anyway, I started the list with "2 homes." I think the next thing on the list was "2 cars." And yes, I continued agreeing with myself very strongly—one is needed, but two would certainly be luxury. Next, "2 TVs." Same thing. And the list went on.

At some point it was as if the still small voice was calling out to me, "Edmunds."

"What?"

"When did you stop saying *luxury?*"

I hadn't realized I'd quit. But I had. Knowing I was going to learn something about myself that would not be entirely a "proud moment," I started back up the list. The point at which I quit saying two of something would be a luxury was the very point on the list where *I* began having two. It was probably "2 phones."

I became aware that I was trying to justify and explain how two phones—and other things further on down the list—were not *really* luxuries. But I kept being hit with the realization that the little rhyme was true in my very own life: "There, there, little luxury, don't you cry—you'll be a necessity by and by."

Is this little exercise relative? Could I say, for example, that two bathrooms are definitely a luxury, whereas the family with five daughters would say, "No way!"

Actually, what finally happened to me was that I realized it's *all* luxury. So many of the things on the list, as I carefully considered them, would be considered luxuries by millions of people in the world: 2 meals in a day, 2 friends, 2 pair of shoes. It is a luxury to have running, safe water in my home—and to be able to make it either hot or cold. It's a luxury to have electricity—to have lights and refrigeration, and a way to make the home warm when it's cold outside, and cool when it's hot. It's a luxury to have even *one* radio or TV or telephone or book, *one* light or bed or . . .

It seems that before we set our hearts too much on anything, we ought to carefully evaluate how happy those people are who already seem to have "everything." What has your experience been? Are those who are the richest in worldly things the happiest people you've ever met? Are they content? Do they enjoy what they have?

In my experience, many *do* enjoy what they have, and they generously share. But some of the most generous (and content) people I have ever known have been those who seemed to have the least in the way of necessities, let alone luxuries.

I think of Rica, a wonderful woman who helped us while I was on my first mission in the Philippines. She was so tiny but did so much help to us. I think we could not have accomplished much without her doing the laundry, going to the market, fixing us food, and helping clean our place. Without her we'd have had to do everything ourselves, and there wouldn't have been much time left for missionary work!

Rica lived with her three children, two daughters and a son, near a river. Her home was very small and very simple. As I remember, she was a widow, raising her children alone. During the time she was with us, she joined the Church. What a happy time that was! She continues to be a faithful member of the Church.

In 1964 there was a terrible volcano with subsequent fires and flooding. Many had been killed, and many were homeless and suffering. Rica came to our home to say, "We should be helping these poor people—we are members of Jesus' church!"

She then showed that she'd brought two things to share: a bucket and a pair of her son's pants. She explained that someone could use the bucket to haul water, and that Johnny had two pair of pants, "and he only needs one."

Does it strike you that this was like the parable of the widow's mite? We had thought she was poor, yet she found something she could share. I have thought sometimes, thinking back on this profound example of a spiritually rich person sharing of her abundance, that even if all I have *ever* given were to be added up, it likely would not be the equivalent of a bucket and a pair of Johnny's pants. Especially when I think of the spirit of absolute love and generosity with which Rica gave them.

Dear reader, do *you* have a bucket and a pair of pants that you might share?

In King Benjamin's remarkable message in the Book of Mormon, we are taught that we can say in our hearts, "If I had I would give" (Mosiah 4:24). But we have to *mean it*. It has to be the true feeling and desire of our hearts.

I'm aware that sometimes I change this a little and think that "if I had what *others* have, I would give." I look at people who have more money, more time, more talents, more of other resources, and I convince myself that if I had all those blessings, I would give more. And I may even try to judge whether those other people are giving what they should be.

One of my brothers gave me a newspaper article many years ago that reported on a survey done of people who worked along or near Wall Street in New York City. The survey was given to a number of people who made around $500,000 a year. Those doing the research wanted to find out one thing: Were these people happy?

Perhaps you can guess the answer: They were not. They were not happy because they were not satisfied because they knew people who were making *more* than $500,000 a year— people who had more stuff and things.

I couldn't believe it! People making $500,000 a year who were not happy? What was *wrong* with them? The big babies! What whiners! Imagine, not being able to be happy and satisfied with that much money. Disgusting! What were they thinking?

Could you get along on $500,000 a year? Wouldn't you like a chance to try? Oh, thought I, if *I* were making $500,000 a year, *I'd* be happy! If someone would just include me in some kind of test or experiment. . . . Think of the tithing! (I put that in in case anyone who could do something about it was watching and/or listening.) *I'd* be happy! *I'd* be satisfied! I'd be *thrilled!* I'd be content and grateful and generous and . . .

But wait! The "Theory of Relativity" came into my mind once again, and I remembered that Sukiman made around $150 a year. It was in fact a little less than that, but I've "rounded it up" for comparing.

Let's suppose Sukiman found out that last year you earned $15,000. I'm pretty sure he wouldn't be able to comprehend it (not nearly as well as we can comprehend $500,000). He likely would even wonder why anyone would need or want that much money—what they'd do with it. He wouldn't be upset with us (like I felt about the folks who were making $500,000), but he might be puzzled if he found out we weren't satisfied or happy. He might somehow realize how much $15,000 could do.

"If I had I would give." I *do* have. If I'm not already generous, I think it might not make a whole lot of difference if I were to have $500,000 or even more—I might just think of more stuff and things I *needed* and never have any left over for sharing.

What does it take for a heart to be generous? Money? Stuff and things? Or is it perhaps a different kind of "heart condition"? Wanting less is probably a better blessing than having more. It really is a condition of our hearts, our desires.

I saw a cartoon once that showed two homeless women sitting on a park bench on what looked to be a cold, wintry day. They were huddled together in the cold. One asked the other, "What are you thinking about?" The response: "I'm thinking of all the nice warm coats the rich women are going to be giving us in July."

Ouch. Do I just give away my leftovers? And do I wait to give them away at a time when I couldn't possibly need or use them anymore? How would it make me feel if I were to give away something I still liked, could still use, and maybe even needed? What if someone out there needed it even more than I did?

The "Theory of Relativity" states that there will *always* be lots of people who have much, much more stuff than we do. Conversely, there will always be millions—and likely *billions*—of Heavenly Father's children who have much, much less than we do, and much less than they desperately need.

Statistics can teach us more about how blessed we are and how much others struggle. I have seen it estimated that about one-third of the world's population goes to bed hungry every night. Realizations like that made me stop saying something I had said so often: "I'm *starving!*" Anyone looking at me would know instantly that I am *far* from "starving." I used to use the word quite loosely, but I don't anymore.

One of the most horrific statistics I've heard is an estimate that between 40,000 and 42,000 little children under the age of five die *every day* in this world from preventable causes.

Ouch! Just *think* of it! Here are little ones, coming to the earth to receive their physical bodies and experience mortality, and for thousands of them there isn't much joy or happiness—there's just hunger and disease and then death, usually from something like diarrhea. The underlying cause is malnutrition in many cases—the little bodies aren't nourished well enough to fight what comes along. And they've not had the chance to be immunized.

I think of this particular statistic and wonder why it doesn't shock us more. I was at one time imagining what it would be like if all 40,000 of these little people were on a ship (and yes, it would have to be a *huge* ship), and the ship sank. We'd be horrified! We'd feel absolutely terrible, and wonder what we could do. But I guess it's one of those relentless statistics, perhaps hard to comprehend and difficult to worry about.

Statistics don't move me as much as people do. If we could know and love even one of those 40,000 little children, it would hurt to see them go away. We'd know that their mothers and fathers wept, just as we would if it were one of our little ones.

I think of my little buddies in Africa and Asia, and I realize that in some ways they've been born in "Never-Never Land." There is so much that they will never, never see, experience, enjoy. Some doesn't matter, but a lot does. There ought to be so much more to life than mere survival.

So here I am sharing all of this information, but why? What are we supposed to do? Are we supposed to give away everything we have, live in a tree, wear a gunny sack, and feel bad for the rest of our lives?

Absolutely not! That's not why I'm sharing these ideas. I'm inviting each of us to consider the notion of rich and poor, and the relativity of our blessings, our needs, our wants, our abundance. I want this chapter to be a reminder of our reasons for being extremely grateful for our blessings, and for becoming more conscious of our other brothers and sisters.

Abundance is what we've been given, and we're not the only ones. The Lord through His prophet Lehi taught that if the people would keep the commandments, they would prosper in the land. King Benjamin reminds us of "the blessed and happy state of those that keep the commandments of God. For behold, they are blessed in all things, both temporal and spiritual" (Mosiah 2:41).

Aren't we rich, not just in temporal blessings but in spiritual ones? We know so much about our relationship to our loving Heavenly Father, and thus about our relationship to each other. How many people in the world know almost nothing about who they are, and who God is? They don't know what a sweet and eternal relationship they have with a God who is their Father in Heaven.

It seems to me that I could learn from that contrast. I could learn of gratitude for knowing who I am, and for a chance to help anyone else know more about who they are, especially with regard to their relationship to their Heavenly Father and their purpose for being on this earth with all the rest of us.

I would like to submit that we're *all* both poor and rich. No one person has *everything*, which means that we all need each other. Think of all the ways we can bless and enrich each other if we're aware of and willing to share our richness.

Usually we measure "rich" and "poor" from the perspective of temporal possessions, but there are other ways to be both rich and poor—other ways to consider and measure.

A few days after we had left Africa in April of 1985, Ann and I had the privilege of visiting the man who made the child health project possible in Eket. Cecilia, one of our African friends, referred to him as "the Big Man." It's a term of respect, not size. And she's right to give him that honored title, because he *is* a "big man"; he has a good heart and has helped to make a difference in the world through his generosity.

He had invited us to his beautiful home in the San Francisco area so that we could report on how the project was going. We even had slides to show him. It was a wonderful, positive visit.

One thing that struck both me and Ann was the difference between his home and Cecilia's. We had so recently been in and around her neat and tidy hut, and now we were in a very genuine palace of a home. It wasn't just that it was about 100 times larger than Cecilia and Samuel's home, it was the wonderful things in it like electricity and running, safe water.

We were intrigued by *everything*—the marble throughout, the white Steinway grand piano, the gold fixtures in the bathrooms, the many TVs and phones, the elevator, and on and on. There was also a state-of-the-art alarm system (which was turned off the night we stayed there, thankfully—I'm sure one of us would have set it off accidentally).

Much of our presentation focused on Cecilia and her accomplishments, as she was the first teacher chosen to work in the child health project and worked so hard to translate materials and train other teachers.

At some point in our visit, our kind host asked more about Cecilia. "Is she a religious person?" "Yes," we responded, "she's very religious." At the time she was the Primary president in our branch. We wondered why he asked. He said, "I think she's very worried about me." We wondered about that, too, and he explained that almost always, when a missionary couple came back from Nigeria, they brought him a letter from Cecilia. And, indeed, she had sent one with us to give to him.

He told us that in every letter he received from her she told all about the Church and the gospel. "She tells me about Jesus, and about Joseph Smith, and about your Book of Mormon—I think she's worried because I'm not a member of your church!"

125

And it hit me: Who's rich? And who's poor? At first glance, the Big Man seems to be the rich one. But think of the ways in which Cecilia is rich as well. Both are willing and desirous of sharing their riches. Each could be more whole by accepting the other's gift. What a powerful, profound lesson this was to me! I say again that, relatively speaking, we're *all* both rich and poor.

Cecilia was eventually called as district Relief Society president, and at this time is president of the Qua River Stake Relief Society. And she and Samuel were present in February of 1998 when President Gordon B. Hinckley addressed a group of 14,400 eager listeners in Port Harcourt, Nigeria, about an hour away from Eket. I'm sure she felt very rich indeed on that day.

Let me tell you about some other rich people I've met in the world. One day in our branch in Central Java, Indonesia, a wonderful member named Ibu Moelyono came to me with excitement, saying, "We have set a goal!" This surprised me, because it's not easy to set goals in developing areas. Life pretty much dictates what you will do and when, and few people have much money.

But I asked with enthusiasm, "What is your goal?" She said, "We're going to the temple!" Once again it caught me off guard. I knew that the average annual income for these friends in our branch would amount to about $150 in U.S. currency. I knew that the closest temple at the time was in Japan. I didn't know what to say, so I didn't say anything. Wise choice.

"Oh, Sister, we have figured out that if we sell everything in our home we don't need [and I'd been to their home, and I pictured it in my mind and wondered what on earth they had to sell], and if we save every Rupiah we possibly can, we'll be able to go in *fifty-five years*."

By then I had kind of a lump in my throat, and I continued

to keep quiet, fighting the tears a bit. Then she added, "Oh, Sister, I hope we'll still be alive—we'll be 110!"

It makes me wonder if I come close to appreciating the privilege of going to the temple so often, and of having so many of them so close.

I suppose I was thinking we should raise money so the Moelyono family could go to the temple. I know there are *many* families just like them, though, who are just as anxious to receive their endowments and be sealed together forever. And thus I rejoice in the building of many more temples, closer to all the faithful Saints, so that they may have the privilege to go to the House of the Lord and receive the ordinances, the joy, and the great blessings waiting for them there.

Ours is the opportunity to make generous contributions so that this can happen. I remember attending the dedication of the Mount Timpanogos Temple in October 1996 and hearing President Hinckley ask us to be faithful in the payment of tithes and offerings so that we'd be able to build more temples as quickly as possible. I think the day is here!

What then shall we do? What shall we do with our abundance, our blessings, and the ways in which we are rich?

I want to share the impressions Heavenly Father has given to me through the Holy Ghost when I've had soul-searching experiences in my prayers, wondering what He wants me to do because of the abundance of blessings I continue to receive.

ENJOY

When I share the first impression that came into my mind, you will likely be thinking, "Isn't that just like our Heavenly Father—wanting us to be happy?" The first impression was to *enjoy!* "Enjoy what I have shared with you!" And I try to do that. I try not to get so accustomed to the wonderful things in life that I forget to enjoy them. When you have a chance, read again Doctrine and Covenants, section 59, and be reminded of how much our Heavenly Father loves to bless us.

APPRECIATE

The next impression was to *appreciate* what He has shared so abundantly with me. I need to remember that all I have is really His, not mine. This helps me to thank Him with all my heart for such rich and wonderful blessings, and to consider them to be "on loan."

Elder Neal A. Maxwell said: "God experiences a deep, divine disappointment in us when we are ungrateful and when we are unwilling to confess God's hand in all things. But it is because of what our sustained ingratitude does to us, not to Him. It . . . represents a profound spur to selfishness and self-centeredness. It is these faults which lead to the celebration of the appetites rather than of spiritual things" (*The Neal A. Maxwell Quote Book*, ed. Cory H. Maxwell [Salt Lake City: Bookcraft, 1997], p. 147).

We probably all need to work to *appreciate* more than we *expect*. Do you know what I mean? I *expect* the sun to come up in the morning—I too seldom thank Heavenly Father for the wonder and blessing of sunshine. I *expect* water to come out of a tap when I turn it on. When it doesn't, I sure can scream! But how often have I expressed thanks for water?

President Brigham Young said, "I do not know of any, excepting the unpardonable sin, that is greater than the sin of ingratitude" (*Discourses of Brigham Young*, comp. John A. Widtsoe [Salt Lake City: Deseret Book, 1978], p. 228).

SHARE

The next impression that came to me was to *share*. And the idea was to share *generously*. Of course! As we try to become more like our Heavenly Father and the Savior, we will naturally become increasingly generous in sharing from our abundance of heavenly blessings.

Is it possible that we could even be more careful in our use of things like water and food, thus letting our Heavenly Father know that we hope we can share with some who may be hungry and thirsty? I believe He will acknowledge such an effort, and will rejoice that we've "caught on."

And oh, the blessing of sharing the *living water* with others, so that in the spiritual sense they never have to thirst again!

SIMPLIFY

Another idea comes from a bumper sticker I once saw: "Live simply so that others may simply live."

When my father passed away in 1997, just after Christmas, we honored the requests he had made for keeping things simple. He had told us, and had written specifically, that he felt too much money was spent on funerals—people seemed to try to have the biggest and best casket, the most flowers, and so on. He said it made him sad that so many went in debt—sometimes for the rest of their lives—just to pay for a funeral.

He had asked that he be buried in a plain pine box with one rose on the top, so that's what we did. He also asked that people not spend money on flowers for him, so the last line of his obituary read, "Please, in lieu of flowers, take your family to dinner." I love it. That's the way our parents are, and that's the example they've set for us.

I waste too much. I'm too careless. I have much more than I need. Take clothing, for example. If I were to put on everything I own and then tip over, I'd never be able to get up! And yet I'm the one who stands in front of a closet so full of clothing that I could hardly add a piece of tissue, and I say, "I don't have anything to wear!" Oh, my.

So I go to my closet with the plan that "*this* time I'm *really* going to give things away! *This* time I'm going to have *lots* of room and empty hangers!" And what happens? I keep coming across things that I haven't worn in a long, long time, and I think (again), "Oh, I *know* I'll be able to wear this again someday, either before or after I die. . . ." And I leave it there. Why is it so hard for me to part with things?

Sometimes I come across something that I realize I'm

emotionally attached to. It's *hard* to give it away! Here's an idea: Take a picture! I've done that, and it works very well. Photos are easier to store, and then the items can be given for others to use.

Even more helpful is a question that comes into my mind as I'm going through things: "Edmunds, is there a chance that there's someone who needs this more than you do?" Almost every single time, the answer is "Yes!" Why should things remain in my closet, my basement, my drawers, or my garage when there's someone who could use and appreciate what I'm keeping "just because"?

LIVE THE GOSPEL

I suppose what I'm saying is that we can live the gospel of Jesus Christ more fully, with all our hearts, paying attention to opportunities we have to become more like the Savior through reaching out to others (see Matthew 25:34–40). We have taken upon us His name, and we can all figure out wonderful ways to be better Christians.

I like the way it's expressed in one of our handbooks:

When we have love in our hearts, we do not need to be told all the ways in which we should care for the poor and needy. . . . There are no limits to what a person may freely offer. . . . [As] we begin to reach out to those who are less fortunate, we will become more conscious of their needs. We will become more compassionate and eager to relieve the suffering of those around us. We will be guided by the Spirit of the Lord to know whom to serve and how to best meet their needs. The Lord taught, "By this shall all men know that ye are my disciples, if ye have love one to another" (John 13:35). The measure of our love for the Lord is the love we show to our fellow-men by serving and blessing them in their times of need. (*Providing in the Lord's Way* [Salt Lake City: The Church of Jesus Christ of Latter-day Saints, 1990], p. 9)

We can keep our covenants, including those in which we

promised to bear one another's burdens so they would be light, and to mourn with those who mourned, and comfort those who were in need of comfort (see Mosiah 18:8–11).

We can more fully keep the covenants we make in temples and in those quiet moments when we talk things over with our Heavenly Father and pour out to Him our deepest desires to become more what and who we ought to be.

Probably most of us can spend less time and money on things we don't really need. We can decrease both our needs and our wants and thus share more from our abundance, as we're asked to do (see D&C 104:18). We can more fully live the law of the fast, which is one way to come closer to consecration (see Isaiah 58).

We can help and love and serve those who are right among us—those in our own home and family, our neighborhood, our branch or ward, at work, at school, or anywhere. Sometimes we may be waiting for a chance to serve and help in a huge, visible way, or in a faraway place. But there are many right around us who hunger and thirst for friendship, attention, and someone to care.

Thinking of hymn number 219, I sometimes sing, "Because I have been given much, I have a lot." I forget the real message of the hymn—that because I have been given much, *I too must share. I must.* My salvation is tied to my willingness to share.

One way I've tried to explain this is to make a chart that has four boxes, set up looking kind of like a baseball diamond. Make the four boxes at "home plate," "first base," and so on, and then write in each box thus:

In the home-plate box, write, "Those who have give." In the first-base box, write, "Those who need receive." In the second-base box, write, "Those who receive work." And in the third-base box, write, "Those who work have."

Look at this diagram as a circle and a cycle. We might say

that those in the home-plate box are rich, and those in the first-base box are poor. But the *process* of giving and receiving exalts both the givers and the receivers (see D&C 104:14–17).

As President Marion G. Romney expressed it: "There is an interdependence between those who have and those who have not. The process of giving exalts the poor and humbles the rich. In the process, both are sanctified" (*Ensign*, November 1982, p. 93).

I know that the gospel of Jesus Christ has the answer to every unmet need in this world. I know that we need each other—that we are interdependent. I know that for every struggle we have, for every single one of our unmet needs, every way in which we are poor, there is someone else who can help—lifting us, blessing us, sharing with us.

I know that there will come a time when everything that is *relative* will become *absolute*. I must prepare now so that I may be absolutely clean and pure, absolutely good, grateful, kind, and sanctified, that I may be worthy and prepared to live with God once more.

I love hymn number 241, the "Count your many blessings" hymn. Read again the words of the third verse:

> When you look at others with their lands and gold,
> Think that Christ has promised you His wealth untold.
> Count your many blessings; money cannot buy
> Your reward in heaven nor your home on high!

I think it's wonderful that we don't "buy our way" to heaven. Our home on high doesn't have an earthly price tag on it. And thank goodness, or perhaps some who deserved most to be there couldn't afford it.

But they *will* be there. And oh, how I hope I can become as rich as Sukiman, Cecilia, Rica, and two little girls covered with clean boards on a cold winter's night! I want to be their neighbors. I want to be where they'll be. And I want to be *comfortable* being near such saints.

May we pray for Sukiman and all the others—those next door, those down the street, those over the ocean, those in our own homes. May we enjoy, appreciate, and share such that one day God can call *us* Zion because we'll be of one heart and one mind, dwelling together in righteousness, and we won't have any who are poor among us (see Moses 7:18). May we find true happiness in cultivating humble, grateful hearts.

Chapter 8

HUMOR AND A HAPPY HEART

THERE HAVE BEEN MANY TIMES in my life when I've been asked, "How did you get your sense of humor? Have you always been funny?" I don't know how to answer that. Humor—seeing the inconsistencies and funny things around me—seems to have been inside of me as long as I can remember. It's part of my life.

Interestingly, when I've been asked about humor, I have many times responded with tears as I've tried to explain. To me, humor is one of the most tender things in life. That may surprise many who are reading and/or who know me. But that's the way I feel. Humor is unifying in a unique way, and tears and laughter blend into each other so many times because the emotions that bring them are so close to each other.

A *sense* of humor is what I mean when I speak of humor. Have you noticed that sometimes when your feelings are tender, or you're sad, or you're "ticked off," you aren't too excited to have someone around who's *too* cheerful? It can be so annoying! This is where the part about sensitivity comes in. Those who seem to have a *sense* of humor really are sensitive, and they have an ability to know when it isn't appropriate to be too "funny." Rather, they can help bring someone out of a bad mood if they handle it right, with sensitivity.

When I speak of humor and the joy of laughing together, then, I want to explain that I do *not* attempt to find humor in every situation or circumstance. There are some people who seem to be on the alert to make every single comment, experience, or moment into a joke. I get weary of such an approach almost instantly, because there is so much in life that just is *not* funny. There are many occasions when it seems inappropriate to try to laugh, when we should be reverent, quiet, empathetic, or compassionate. I enjoy the opportunity to be serious with others—to speak of things that matter most and that are sacred and holy. And I'm very much aware of the counsel to let the solemnities of eternity rest upon our minds (see D&C 43:34).

So I don't want this chapter to be a collection of "My Favorite Jokes," or the sharing of a bunch of experiences that I think will make others laugh. I hope other parts of this book will help with that. Instead, in this chapter I would like to explore the notion of humor and laughter, cheerfulness and optimism. I want to speak of that which brings us closer together, breaks down barriers, and lessens the chance that we'll miss opportunities to lift and cheer one another. I want to share ideas on the connection between good humor and a happy heart.

To me, a good sense of humor is a way to keep from being too pretentious, too perfect, or too isolated or insulated from others. It's a kind of honesty in looking at ourselves and all that surrounds us. Humor for me is often two parts love and three parts courage. There are times when it can keep us from allowing pride to creep into our hearts and behavior. Humor can be—and should be—gentle and kind, bringing down walls that may separate us, but never used as a "weapon" to hurt or humiliate. This, in part, is what I mean by a *sense* of humor, or wholesome humor.

A good sense of humor can help us control our temper, "back off" when a situation is getting too tense, and "hold our tongue" when we might say something we would later regret, something that might wound another's heart and cause us to feel ashamed and sorry.

A wholesome sense of humor includes the ability to know how to be sensitive to situations and to others' feelings. Humor is laughing *with* people, but never *at* them. Humor is learning to laugh at ourselves and circumstances, but never at that which is sacred. Humor is a way to deal with life's inconsistencies without irreverence.

Often my own humor seems to be an acknowledgment of my weaknesses, and thus a way to help me continue striving to do better and be better. It's a way for me to be *real*, to be genuine and honest in sharing my thoughts and feelings with others. It helps me avoid something I have earnestly sought to stay away from: hypocrisy.

Once when I was thinking a lot about humor as a way to be genuine, I ran across this description of President Wilford Woodruff recorded by Matthias F. Cowley: "By nature he was an unsuspicious man and that made his life free from the jealousies, envies, and misgivings so destructive of human happiness. That nature made him an optimist. He went about life not only looking for the good, but with ability to see it. He had nothing to conceal, nothing to disfigure, therefore the shades and colorings of life with him were true to nature" (*Wilford Woodruff, History of His Life and Labors* [Woodruff Family Association, 1909], pp. 647–48). Wouldn't that be a pleasant way to live?

In connection with humor's contribution to happiness, I've also done a lot of thinking about how humor relates to reverence for that which is holy and sacred, and the difference between light-mindedness and lightheartedness. Is there a place in our lives for happy laughter? Is there a place for appropriate humor in the Church and the gospel?

Elder Bruce R. McConkie wrote about this in his book *Mormon Doctrine*, under the title "Light-mindedness":

> In connection with his command to build a house of God and conduct a school of the prophets therein, the Lord commanded his ministers to cease from light speeches, laughter, and light-mindedness. (D. & C. 88:121.) Obviously the elders of Israel, while engaged on the Lord's solemn and sober business, must avoid those trifling and frivolous things which make up light-mindedness. Theirs is an awesome responsibility while so engaged, for they are dealing with the souls of men. The divine injunction here given is not to be construed to enjoin proper and wholesome relaxation and recreational activities. These latter have the Lord's approval. (D. & C. 136:28.) (*Mormon Doctrine*, 2nd ed. [Salt Lake City: Bookcraft, 1966], p. 446)

In September 1985, Elder M. Russell Ballard told the missionaries at the Missionary Training Center in Provo, Utah: "Light-mindedness *offends*." As I wrote that comment in my notes, I thought, "That's it!" He then said to the missionaries, "You can tell." You can, can't you? You can tell when something is inappropriate (or, as I sometimes put it, "senseless," as in, "not a real sense of humor" or "without sensitivity").

Elder Ballard added, "If we said you couldn't have a sense of humor, all the Brethren would be in jeopardy." In the times when I've had the privilege of being in the presence of Church leaders and others whom I admire, I have come to feel that those with great spirituality also seem to have a keen sense of humor and a great capacity to enjoy life and relationships.

Elder Neal A. Maxwell has expressed the thought that "Humor as a reflection of the incongruities of life can be helpful. The living prophets I have known have all had such a sense of humor" (*Deposition of a Disciple* [Salt Lake City: Deseret Book, 1976], p. 52).

One of the things that endears President Gordon B. Hinckley to me is his wonderful, appropriate *sense* of humor. He *senses* when something is funny, and he helps me see things more clearly with his happy and positive way of sharing.

One little but typical example occurred on Saturday, October 6, 1990. I was in the Tabernacle for general conference, and President Hinckley, then a counselor in the First Presidency, was conducting. Elder Eduardo Ayala had just spoken, and he had an obvious Spanish accent. President Hinckley stood up afterward and said, smiling, "I wish I could speak Spanish as well as he speaks English!"

With that one tender statement he had us smiling and understanding. He used himself and his inability to speak Spanish as a way of complimenting Elder Ayala, who perhaps found it a daunting challenge to use a second language to express his deepest thoughts about the gospel of Jesus Christ with thousands watching and listening.

Oh, how I want to discover, develop, and share the kind of sense of humor President Hinckley has! He never uses it to put someone down. There is no sarcastic edge to that which he shares. Who can ever forget President Hinckley's unique and incredible way of deflecting the praise Elder Russell M. Nelson had given him in a conference talk on October 4, 1997, by challenging him to a duel in the basement of the Tabernacle "right after this meeting."

And then toward the close of the session he said something like, "Brother Nelson, I've repented. Thank you for your kind words. We'll postpone the duel." How can you not love such a prophet with all your heart for his ability and willingness to be so real, so happy, so faithful?

He uses humor to unify us, as when he said, on a day when it was very warm in the Tabernacle and we were almost all fanning ourselves, that he knew we were hot, but we weren't as hot as we were going to be if we didn't repent! The happy laughter throughout the Tabernacle was evidence of a unique moment of unity and shared understanding.

In the October 1984 general conference, he invited us: "Be happy in that which you do. Cultivate a spirit of gladness in your homes. Subdue and overcome all elements of anger, impatience, and unbecoming talk one to another. Let the light of the gospel shine in your faces wherever you go and in whatever you do" (*Ensign*, November 1984, p. 86).

This wonderful prophet and leader has helped me understand much more about why humor, gladness, happiness, and optimism are such important and treasured outcomes of doing our best to live the gospel of Jesus Christ. He also helps me understand why humor must always be gentle, sensitive, and appropriate.

To me he is an example of everything he teaches, including the way the light of the gospel shines in his face wherever he goes and in whatever he does. And he invites us to follow! Speaking at a multistake fireside for youth in St. Louis, Missouri, he said: "Be happy. I'm not pleading for long faces and dour looks or misery. I'm pleading for smiles and laughter and fun and good times. Choose the right" (*Church News*, 6 November 1993).

Can you think of the difference in yours or another's countenance between "dour looks" and the light of the gospel shining through? As stated in Proverbs 15:13, "A merry heart maketh a cheerful countenance." And President Joseph Fielding Smith counseled: "I do not believe the Lord intends and desires that we should pull a long face and look sanctimonious and hypocritical. I think he expects us to be happy and of a cheerful countenance" (Conference Report, October 1916, p. 70).

I'm a "people watcher," and it makes me feel sad when I see

someone with a "long face," as President Smith described it. I find I want to say or do something to turn those frowns upside down, giving their wearers reason to "smile all the while." Do you find, as I do, that it's very inviting and attractive to notice someone's countenance reflecting a sense of peacefulness and good cheer?

A wholesome sense of humor in the context of the gospel of Jesus Christ can give us a way of looking at ourselves and life—and all that is around us—in a healthy, positive way. This attribute of cheerfulness, of genuine happiness, can carry us over and through a whole lot of adversity and trouble. It can help us appreciate and express what is genuinely funny, and to share such observations in appropriate times and ways.

Often, good humor can help us bend instead of break, smile instead of cry (although there's nothing wrong and a whole lot right about a good cry), and come to an understanding that we ought not to take ourselves *too* seriously all the time.

Elder Neal A. Maxwell has said: "The true believer is serious about the living of his life, but he is of good cheer. His humor is the humor of hope and his mirth is the mirth of modesty—not the hollow laughter or the cutting cleverness of despair. Unlike those of a celebrated 'devil-may-care' lifestyle, his is the quiet 'heaven-does-care' attitude" (*The Neal A. Maxwell Quote Book*, ed. Cory H. Maxwell [Salt Lake City: Bookcraft, 1997], p. 166).

"Life is really a battle between fear and faith, pessimism and optimism," taught President Hugh B. Brown. "Fear and pessimism paralyze men with skepticism and futility. One must have a sense of humor to be an optimist in times like these. . . . But your good humor must be real, not simulated. Let your smiles come from the heart and they will become contagious. . . . Men [or women] without humor tend to forget their source, lose sight of their goal, and with no lubrication in their mental crankshafts, they must drop out of the race" (*The Abundant Life* [Salt Lake City: Bookcraft, 1965], p. 50).

When I first read that quotation from President Brown, I realized that one thing humor has done for me in my life is to help me remain positive and avoid pessimism. I agree with him that one must have a sense of humor to be an optimist with all that is so terrible and sad and evil in our time. I also agree that a smile that comes from the heart can be contagious. In my very unscientific studies and observations, it has occurred to me that smiles can be every bit as contagious as yawns!

Elder Richard L. Evans shared the thought that "Humor is essential to a full and happy life. It is a reliever and relaxer of pressure and tension, and the saving element in many situations" (*Improvement Era*, February 1968, p. 71).

Has it been that way for you, as it has for me so many times? Can you think of situations where it could have "gone either way"? Do you remember moments when humor really has been the saving element in an otherwise awful or embarrassing or frightening situation?

I remember once when I was working as a nurse, I was assigned a patient who was described as "an old grouch." Apparently he was completely negative, wouldn't smile, and very seldom said anything to anyone. He never thanked any of the staff for their efforts to help him or show kindness. He just lay in his bed frowning and muttering.

I took this as a challenge, and approached him with all kinds of optimism. I was so sure I could reach him! But I couldn't seem to. I would say I tried *everything*, but I've quit using that word as often as I used to—I feel that the Spirit has more ideas than we could use in a lifetime, let alone in one moment, one situation, or one relationship!

I didn't exactly feel frustrated, but I felt sad for the old grouch—he was missing so much by closing himself off to others. I felt like singing a little song I'd learned in Primary, which starts out "No one likes a frowny face," but I didn't want to make fun of him or add to whatever was causing such sustained unhappiness.

Then I got an idea. I went in his room and got right up close, "in his face," and I smiled a dazzling smile (enhanced by my ten years in braces as a child!) and said with all sincerity and fervor, "Sir, I know you are *extremely* happy to have me as your nurse. I know you like me a *lot*, and you're just trying to think of a way to tell me!"

I saw him try not to smile. I had reached him! He was a goner! I said something like, "Thank you for enjoying me so much. I enjoy you, too." And I left. I didn't want to seem to be waiting for him to respond, to put him on the spot.

From that moment on we had a wonderful and happy time. I found out he was just lonely, shy, and frightened. How many times is that true? How many times is it possible to use a little humor (which is often a way of having the courage to be honest) to help break down a barrier?

I remember once when I had finished speaking in another state at a Relief Society meeting, I was leaving a chapel, and I was doing a lot of hugging. I was holding my books and stuff in my left arm, so I was saying things about giving "one-armed hugs." One cheerful sister approached me and I gave her my very best hug, making my typical comment about it being one-armed. Then I realized she had only one arm!

I have always tried to use the kind of humor that didn't embarrass anyone or make them feel awkward or hurt. Here was a moment when I wasn't sure what to do or say, though. What came out of my mouth was an absolutely honest expression: "Oh! You're an *expert!*" And she laughed with delight and we had a wonderful conversation about the challenges of having just one arm.

What comfort it was to me that she responded with good humor! She seemed to realize I would never have wanted to make her feel bad or seem to be making fun of what must have been a great frustration to her.

You're aware, as I am, that "studies have shown" (don't you love that phrase—it's as if it makes everything that follows credible, accurate, and true, and the speaker is wearing a white lab coat and a serious expression, peering over dark-rimmed glasses) that the writer of Proverbs had it correct: "A merry heart doeth good like a medicine: but a broken spirit drieth the bones" (Proverbs 17:22). A similar message appears just a little earlier: "A merry heart maketh a cheerful countenance: but by sorrow of the heart the spirit is broken" (Proverbs 15:13).

Good humor and laughter are therapeutic. When people laugh hard, the heart rate speeds up, the circulatory system is stimulated, and muscles go limp. The body's immune system is stimulated, and more endorphins, which are natural pain-relieving substances in the brain, are produced. No wonder a merry heart doeth good like a medicine!

It has been my experience that the medicine is not just for the one who's merry, either. Do you like to be around people who are cheerful and optimistic? Do you find you feel better when you're with them? It's certainly that way for me!

Think of someone you enjoy being around. Think of someone who lifts your spirits and lightens your burdens. Would you describe that person as being happy? Does he or she tend to have a good sense of humor? Does the person help you laugh when you need to?

I remember how sad I felt after our daddy went Home just after Christmas in 1997. Some time after that, when I was getting ready to go on a trip for a speaking assignment, my sister Charlotte gave me an envelope and told me not to open it until I got to the airport. When I looked in the envelope I discovered a sweet note along with about thirty of her favorite cartoons that she's saved through the years. I laughed and cried as I went through each one and reread her note several times. Her gesture was even more important than the cartoons she shared. She wanted to lift my spirits. She wanted to help me bear my burden. And she lightened it in such a significant way.

President Howard W. Hunter had a wonderful sense of humor. On the day he passed away, his close friend for twenty-three years, Jon M. Huntsman, shared some memories in an interview with Mike Cannon of the *Church News*. Brother Huntsman lived in the same ward as President Hunter and served for nearly nine years as his stake president. He also had opportunities to travel with the prophet and was one of the speakers at his funeral. In the *Church News* interview, Brother Huntsman told several happy stories of experiences he'd shared with the prophet.

> He told about being together in a foreign country and having been served spoiled meat at a formal dinner in a stately location. The two men each took a bite and thought better of it, hiding the rest of the meat as best they could to be respectful. Several months later, President Hunter was hospitalized. Seriously ill, he lapsed into a coma. Brother Huntsman and Elder M. Russell Ballard stopped by for a visit. Leaning over the unresponsive prophet's bedside, Brother Huntsman spoke in a rather loud voice: "'President, I love you very much. I love you so much that I brought some of that good meat we had together, but unfortunately the dogs ate it on the way to the hospital.' He broke out in such loud laughter that the nurses down the hall came running into his room, and within a couple of hours he came out of this coma he had been in. The doctors wouldn't say for sure what brought him out of it, but I think he and I both knew that it was just the memory of that horrible meat." (*Church News*, 11 March 1995)

That's another part of good humor that I appreciate so much—the remembering of experiences and circumstances that bring the smiles and happy laughter back as though it had just happened again.

In my life, a sense of humor has helped me in several specific ways. For example, I'm aware that it helps me cut down on competition and envy. It adds to my feelings of contentment. It has brought me an increase in peace and calm. It helps me put many moments in a larger perspective. It helps me handle stress. It helps me go through my deep waters and fiery trials without succumbing to bitterness or discouragement. Humor is almost magical!

Humor helps us hang on and hang in through the normal ups and downs of life: through paper cuts and budget cuts, dark and stormy nights, losing at Monopoly and losing at love, weight gains and heart pains, falling arches and falling stock markets, flat tires and flat chests, broken hearts and broken glasses, days when time flies too quickly and nights when time drags too slowly, smashed thumbs and hopes, slipping on the ice in front of two or a hundred people, spilled jam and traffic jams, and divorce and cancer and single parenthood and . . . and almost anything and everything.

Humor has tied our family closer together. I love sitting around the dinner table with my family and having someone start, "Remember when . . ." and then we laugh. Sometimes we only have to say a phrase or a word and everyone cracks up! I love the memories of so many things we've worked on together, such as unusual letters, skits for a ward party, or some other project.

One incident that is a "family classic" comes to mind. When Dad was a physician in Cedar City, in Southern Utah, he had a particular older woman as a patient who came frequently to his office with her adult son. Neither the mother nor the son seemed completely whole mentally. There were times when their behavior was unusual, as the time when the mother saw Dad on the street and slapped him on the back (with a "Hi, Doc!") so hard that she almost threw him into the ditch.

As I mentioned, this duo came to Dad's office frequently with various complaints, but perhaps mostly wanting someone to pay attention to them. One day when they arrived, Dad's nurse thought she'd be clever, and she sent a note in to Dad saying, "The Queen and the Prince are here." Dad peeked out to see that it was this particular mother and her son, and he wrote something on the note and passed it back to the nurse: "God save the King!"

Some people seem to think that the opposite of humor is spirituality and "seriousness." For me that's like saying faith is the opposite of hope. Why separate two things that belong together and complement each other?

For me, the opposite of good humor is too often contention. The opposite of happiness is misery. The opposite of cheerfulness is gloom. The opposite of optimism is an almost oppressive pessimism. The opposite of a cheerful countenance is too often a frowny face.

Humor can help us avoid constant murmuring and complaining. Good humor is often the very opposite of anger, envy, and self-centeredness. A humorless heart is too often a hard heart and can lead to a stiff neck. Ouch!

Humor has a way of leveling—of helping us to experience equality. When many of us are touched or amused by the same thing, it reaches across a lot of artificial walls and even cuts through language or other communication barriers. I've been in many places where I couldn't speak the language but still seemed to be able to communicate, especially with the children, through humor. I'd pull faces and act silly, and we'd laugh and hug each other and feel very, very close.

Often humor is used to make a serious point. It helps us get things in perspective.

Many people I know who are considered funny are people who weep easily. Perhaps we use humor to cover the tears and prop up the tenderness. I've told friends that I don't feel as "funny" as I used to before I lived in Africa and Asia and came face to face and heart to heart with a lot of suffering and pain. There is so much in this world that is *not* funny. But let's thank God in the coming days for all there is to be happy about and all that gives us genuine reason to rejoice!

I'm convinced that the gospel is good news, that our Heavenly Father's plan is a plan of happiness, and that joy and enjoyment are a large part of a life of goodness and godliness. As Elder Neal A. Maxwell put it, "There is a special gladness that goes with the gospel, and appropriate merriment" (*Things As They Really Are* [Salt Lake City: Deseret Book, 1978], p. xiv).

May we bring happiness to each other. May our Heavenly Father help us to find good humor amidst all that is troubling today. May we look forward with cheerful countenances to the time when Jesus Christ will come again and we will finally rest from all that isn't pleasant or good or kind or real. "And then may God grant unto you that your burdens may be light, through the joy of his Son. And even all this can ye do if ye will. Amen" (Alma 33:23).

Chapter 9

A MERRY HEART DOETH GOOD LIKE A MEDICINE

HAVE YOU EVER HAD A PHONE call that has "changed everything"? I received such a call on the first Sunday of 1993. The year had started off innocently, with no particular hint of what was about to happen.

Earlier that morning, January 3, I had called my mother as usual. Interestingly, we had talked for quite a while about nursing homes. I told of a visit I'd made to an unhappy friend, and I reminded my mother of my promise, "You'll *never* go to a nursing home! Never!" And that morning I added dramatically, but kind of laughingly, "Over my dead body!" She laughed too and said, "It may be over *my* dead body!"

I told her I was serious, and that I would quit work before I'd ever let her or Dad be put in a place like that. She said, "Well, maybe Dad and I will be *praying* to go to a rest home so we can have some rest!" And we laughed and had a good talk.

Such challenges and decisions seemed a long way away. Dad was ninety-one at the time and doing very well, and Mom was "only" seventy-nine and could do anything. She said the two of them were just getting ready to go out and do the chores;

having the horses and donkeys and all the other responsibilities gave them a reason to get up and go out in the mornings. I could hear Dad in the background, putting on his boots, whistling happily.

And so began a beautiful Sunday morning, the first of the year. After some visits, I headed toward the freeway and the airport to pick up a friend returning from the Christmas vacation. I called home on my car phone, keeping in touch as I always did.

My niece Wendy answered, which caught me off guard. It was as if somewhere in my mind an alarm went off: Something's wrong! Wendy said, "Something's happened to Grandma—she's had a stroke or something." Mom had called Wendy about noon but couldn't say anything—she was just making noises. Wendy could tell who it was and alerted her mother, my sister Susan. They live right next door to my parents and went over immediately.

They told me Mom was up and around but was unable to talk to them. She just made unintelligible sounds, trying to form words. Susan said she had called our other sisters and brothers, and they were on their way.

I made other arrangements for my friend at the airport and hurried home. We convinced Mom (against her will) that she needed to go to the hospital. There was a long wait in the emergency room, and a long list of questions to answer. What had happened? Well, Mom had been getting ready to go to church. She had taken a hot bath. When she got out she felt dizzy, and her vision went blurry. She could not yet describe everything except by her own version of sign language, but she knew something was very wrong.

Eventually some test results began to come back. Mom had definitely had a stroke—on the left side, smack in her speech/communication center. She also had some weakness on the right side of her body, but it was minimal, thank goodness. She would have to stay in the hospital for a while.

The bishopric and the Relief Society president arrived at her room on the fourth floor about the same time Mom did. We stayed out of the room so they could have a short visit with her.

They came out in a little while and were laughing—said she'd managed "three hells and a damn." Ha. Those words seemed to express so well the frustration she was feeling. Once the words were out of her mouth she could hear them, and she would laugh along with everyone else. This was *not* her regular vocabulary!

We went into her room. It was hard to see her trying so hard to communicate and not to be able to catch on to what she wanted to say. We worked for over an hour to get the word *elephant*. My youngest brother, Richard, his wife, Glenda, and their sons had gone to the New Year's Day Rose Parade, and they had been excited by the float from Indonesia, which featured live elephants.

Extracting this information from Mom was like playing charades or something. We were asking things like "animal, vegetable, or mineral?" We had narrowed it down to "New Year," "Richard and Glenda," and "Bud men" (which is what we called their four sons), but there was still something else she was trying to say, and we just couldn't come up with it.

Then Dad said "elephant." Mom *screamed* and jumped up in bed. That was what she wanted to tell us! Elephants! Frank laughed and asked Mom why she didn't hold her arms out like a trunk and hum "Jumbo Elephant"—she *was* able to hum tunes. That cracked her up.

And so began the days, the weeks, and the months of Mom's recovery from a stroke. It hasn't been "complete," but it's been remarkable. I'm convinced that her sense of humor—her ability to laugh at herself and circumstances—has been one of the critical factors in her progress. She has helped me understand that "A merry heart doeth good like a medicine" (Proverbs 17:22).

Each of the days I spent at Mom's bedside seemed to be filled with funny experiences along with the worry of what was going to happen. We laughed a lot. I had one of the most extended periods of time in my life for observing "up close and personal" how her cheery nature and depth of happiness and faith would carry her through this experience.

One morning when both Frank and I were there, Mom said she wanted to brush her teeth, so she got up to do so. She put some toothpaste on her finger. I said, "Why did you put it there?" And I picked up the toothbrush, thinking she would put the toothpaste on it. Well, she proceeded to rub the tooth-paste on her nose! Then she happened to look in the mirror. She sighed, shook her head, and then burst out laughing.

Another day, Ann brought gingerbread cookies made in the shapes of Donald Duck and Mickey Mouse. Mom ate Donald's head and pronounced it delicious.

I was constantly amazed at Mom's ability to avoid letting her struggles, especially with trying to speak, get the best of her. As a nurse I had worked with patients who seemed to give up, but not my mother!

Much of our time was spent with Mom trying to get back the ability to express what was on her mind and in her heart. It was a long, slow process, and we both tried hard to be patient. When it was just the two of us in the room, we sometimes sang songs. This seemed to bring words back to her. She especially enjoyed "Give, Said the Little Stream."

We'd go through the days of the week and numbers, and she'd do her best to talk to visitors, staff people, and those who called on the phone. One of Mom's first sentences happened on a morning when John called from Mapleton, where he was spending time with Dad. Mom asked, "What you do?" A sentence! She looked at me with a big smile, her bright blue eyes full of happiness at her accomplishment.

Sometimes Mom and I would go walking in the hall looking at the pictures and having Mom say what everything was. Once when we were on such an adventure, we got to a corner and I pointed left, asking, "What direction is that?" She looked at me funny and said, "Oh, don't you know?" Well, we laughed so hard that a nurse came to see what was happening. She laughed with us, saying how nice it was to have Mom around because she was so cheerful. She was being her usual self: A happifier!

Every day she worked on reading as well as speaking. When flowers or notes would arrive, she'd try to sound out the names and words. One morning she was going over the list of people in her ward, using that as an exercise in recognizing and saying names. She got to one name and studied and pondered the last name—couldn't quite get it, so she went over to the first name. Then she squealed with delight: "Oh! That's *me!*"

One of the first names Mom could say was "Charlotte," so the rest of us immediately began to say that we realized Charlotte was her favorite child among the eight of us. Mine was about the last name to come to her. Too complicated, I guess. She'd call me Charlotte and I'd say, "I'm the *other* Charlotte," and she'd laugh, knowing she didn't have it right yet. She reverted to calling our oldest brother "Baby Paul," as she had during his first few months of life.

Not everything about the stroke and the hospital experience was funny or happy. As I've tried to express in this book, it's my feeling that happiness is not the absence of trials, and having a sense of humor doesn't mean you're never "down."

There were some tender moments, for sure. One morning before Mom was to leave for some tests, she indicated that she'd like to have a prayer. So I shut the door and pulled the curtain. I said, "So whose turn is it?" and she laughed and pointed to me. What a sweet experience we had. It was as if I was prompted about what to say. We could feel Heavenly Father's spirit, and we felt so close to each other at that moment. She kept thanking me. She'd say, "Thank you . . . pear." And I knew she meant, "Thank you for the prayer."

There was great rejoicing and excitement on the day Mom was able to go home. Frank, Charlotte, and Paul helped put sixteen flower arrangements and all of Mom's things in my car. The hospital staff told her they'd miss her, and off we went.

As I drove along, Mom was so happy to see everything—to be outside the hospital. It was a very enjoyable drive. Some funny things happened, including seeing a huge sign that said "Termite and Pest Control." As she'd been doing, she tried to say the words. After a lot of hard work she got "pest." Then "control," and, after we had passed the sign, she said rather quietly, "turd." We laughed at that. She knew it was close but not exactly the right word.

When we got home, the dogs went crazy. I pulled in and went around and opened the door, and they jumped up and licked her face and twirled and were so excited! She was too.

And then we went in the front door, and I realized Dad hadn't heard the noise. He was sitting in his chair. We went up the hall and turned to the living room. I called, "Dad." It was like a Frank Capra movie as he turned and saw Mom and jumped up and hugged and kissed her. Oh, it was so tender!

Mom wanted to write thank-you notes for those who'd sent flowers. On one she wanted me to write "you're the best," but it came out "you're the pits." When we quit laughing we continued with thank-you notes and phone calls.

Mom would sometimes get frustrated because, as she made known, she couldn't "get after" people the way she'd once been able to. She could think of things she wanted to say, but she couldn't make them come out. Once when a man was working in the yard and was apparently sarcastic and short with her, she told me she said something to him like, "If I could talk I would tell you off!" I think he got the message, because after that he was much kinder.

I admit that sometimes I wished she could just snap back to the way she used to be—to talk easily and freely as she always had before. I missed that part of her. At the same time, I felt grateful that she could communicate as well as she did, because I'd had enough experience to know that it could have been a lot worse.

Gradually Mom began doing the familiar things she hadn't done for a while. After she'd been home about a week, she wanted to go out with Dad to do the chores. I happened to be there, and I walked out with her. She seemed especially happy to see her donkeys, and she could say most of their names.

One important thing that happened to us as a result of Mom's stroke was a more serious approach to our family councils. It felt comforting and helpful to have all of us sitting with our parents, discussing and deciding so many specific things.

We worked to make sure Dad could hear everything, which wasn't easy, especially when we'd all be talking at once. John sat by Dad and explained everything the best he could. We wanted both Dad and Mom to have a chance to express their feelings. At some point we were talking about wanting to help so that Mom wouldn't have another stroke. She said it would be okay, and that she wouldn't mind dying. She said, "I'm ready."

One particular day we had a sign-up sheet of things we'd all thought of that needed to be done. One of my responsibilities was to talk to Mom and Dad about their funerals so that when something *did* happen, we'd be able to make plans according to their wishes. After the others left, I sat in the kitchen with Mom. I had the feeling she wanted to talk, and it was true. It touched me deeply as she told me in her halting but understandable way that she'd been doing a lot of soul searching.

She asked if I thought she was a shallow person. She had never asked me anything like that before, but at any point in my life I would have given the same answer: "Absolutely not." She explained that she didn't write poetry or paint, and she wondered what she would be leaving behind. I could tell this was a great concern.

I shared my own feelings about what she would leave behind, and by this time we were both crying. This was a very sacred time. There had not been that many opportunities for me to listen to her pour out her heart.

Often when I'd go to visit, Mom would ask me to help with her homework. One thing she was working on was figuring out what time it was. Numbers had become a real problem. She had a cardboard clock with hands on it, and she'd put them in some position and then say, "Let's see . . . the big hand is on the . . ." with a big smile.

It really did seem like the numbers had become scrambled inside her head. Once when she was trying to think of what time it was, she was saying "30," and then "4," but I could tell that it wasn't what she wanted to say. I guessed: "5:30?" She said "No—the other way." "3:30?" "Yes!" She was trying to explain that she had awakened at 3:30 and couldn't go back to sleep.

We did other kinds of work with numbers, including adding, subtracting, and the hardest of all: multiplying. We worked on writing checks and balancing her checkbook.

Once when I was helping write some checks to pay bills, I made a mistake, and she said immediately something like, "It's good I'm here to help you," and we had a good laugh.

Once when Mom was outside watching some children fly their kites, a neighbor came along and seemed very happy to see her. He asked how she was doing, and they chatted for a few minutes. At some point he asked her how old she was, and she responded, "Oh, I am 100." When she heard it she realized it wasn't right, and they both laughed. After explaining that she didn't remember her numbers, she told him, "I don't know how really much I am!"

She was so much fun. Such a good sport. She almost always laughed first at her mistakes. After this particular incident I would sometimes refer to her as "the 100-year-old woman."

She eventually began making candy again, something for which she had become quite famous and had won many awards. But there were times she'd call laughing because she'd become mixed up on numbers as she was adding ingredients, and the candy didn't turn out quite the way it used to. She hung in there, though, and got back her ability to make some of the best candy anywhere.

She worked hard on reading, too. We'd encourage her to read out loud, thinking this would help her to both see and hear the words. Sometimes when grandchildren were there they'd crawl up beside her in her chair and help her with her reading. They'd help her "sound out" the words she didn't recognize. Precious!

She did a lot of reading on her own. She told me it was easier to read Zane Grey books than the *Ensign* or the scriptures. It seems the stroke scattered words every which way, and she had to concentrate not just on recognizing and pronouncing each single word but on trying to figure out what they meant when put together. She worked for a whole year on reading the Book of Mormon after she had the stroke.

At first Mom was receiving help from a speech therapist, but she eventually quit going. She told us she had told the therapist, "That's stupid," when she asked her to do some exercise. She said, "I not three!" I guess some things seemed silly and like "baby talk" to her. Later she told me, smiling, "I want to learn to speak again—but I don't want to have to work at it."

The more I thought about it, the more I decided, "Well, at seventy-nine, why should she have to do something she doesn't want to do?" It wasn't like she was just sitting around not trying or progressing at all. She'd read notes and letters from people, and she even spent time in the dictionary frequently, reading the words and remembering what they meant.

Once she had made the decision to quit formal speech therapy, she told us she was sleeping much better at night. We didn't know it was putting so much pressure and stress on her.

One morning I called Mom quite early, so she knew it would be me. She picked up the phone and said in her funny, halting way, "Who else but a *nerd* . . ." and we laughed for quite a while.

When she couldn't think of the words she wanted to say, she would find alternatives. For example, she tried to say that Topper, one of the dogs, was barking because Joko, another dog, was blocking the doorway, but she couldn't think of *blocking*. So she said, "Joko has plugged the door."

I told her I thought that was great—that she was able to get her point across and was continually thinking of new vocabulary words. Often when we'd finish talking, either in person or over the phone, she'd say, "Have a day!" This became a greeting that many of us used in place of "Have a nice day."

I loved hearing the way she sometimes mixed things up. She told a granddaughter one day that she'd like to have "strangled eggs," and scrambled eggs have been "strangled eggs" since then.

Some days Mom would indicate that she wanted to visit some neighbors, and off we'd go. I felt good about her getting to a point where she wanted to do that again. One day as we were visiting, a neighbor asked, "Are you going to speech therapy?" "Oh, yes." "Is it helping?" That struck Mom funny and she laughed hard, as did the rest of us.

Mom began calling us and others on the phone a little more frequently as time went by. One day at the MTC I got a message from her, which I saved for a long time so I could listen again and again. She had said, haltingly, "Check your mother." That was all. So I had called her and found out she needed me to get some things for her and Dad on the way home.

Some days I'd feel tired after work, and I'd almost drive straight home. But then I'd stop to spend some time with my parents. One day as I was leaving, Mom said, "You are my ray of sunshine!" Then she smiled and said, "There, how's that?" I told her I liked it a lot! I think she'd been working on it.

Toward the end of February, Mom began having some episodes where she felt she might be having another stroke. This was frightening not only to her but to the rest of us as well. She'd get headaches, she'd feel dizzy, and her vision would be blurred. She'd try to describe to us a feeling of her head being "full."

Often during such episodes her blood pressure would be back up sky high. She'd say things like, "I'd rather *die* than have another stroke! I don't want to be an invalid!" She felt such anxiety about possibly losing completely her ability to communicate and to get around and be independent.

It was hard for me to see the fear in her eyes at such times. I'd feel so helpless! I knew I couldn't just say positive things and have her "snap out of it."

Sometimes she'd talk about wanting to die. Other times she'd say she had a few things she still wanted to do, and she'd like to be around "for a little while longer." One thing that was depressing and discouraging to her was when she'd feel a "setback"—when there was something she couldn't say or do quite as well as she had a few days before.

There were times when Mom worried about her spirituality, because she didn't always feel like going to Church meetings or having the home teachers or visiting teachers come. I tried to assure her that she was not wicked or evil, but very normal, and that she would know what she could and couldn't do.

After the episodes would pass, she would frequently say

something about having wondered, in her low moments, if she'd ever feel like laughing again. But somehow, from the center of her soul and heart, the humor and laughter and optimism would come back to cheer and bless her life and ours.

Once she told me that although she had pretty much quit trying to pray out loud with others listening, she always prayed in her mind. She told me that there was one time when she couldn't think of His name, so she just explained that she needed help, and addressed her prayer to "that Man up there who helps us." I think that worked just fine!

I remember once when Mom was sharing her feelings with me, and the tears came as she said she'd been wondering about Mary and how she felt as she held her little baby Son. She indicated that the scriptures said Mary kept things in her heart, and Mom let me know that she was keeping a lot of her deepest feelings in her heart, and that she had done that most of her life. What a priceless moment to share with her!

One Saturday in the late afternoon I answered the phone and heard someone give a long sigh. I thought it was someone being funny, and I laughed. But then, instantly, I realized it was Mom and she was in terrible distress. She was sobbing, saying, "I can't . . . I need . . . I can't . . ." I went crazy. "I'll be right there, Mom! I'll be right there!" I grabbed some shoes, talking out loud as I ran out the door: "I'll be there, Mom. Hang on!"

I jumped in the car and called Charlotte while I quickly drove the two minutes to Mom and Dad's. I ran in the house and hollered at Dad, who was sitting quietly in his chair, "Where's Mom?" He said, "Oh, I think she's taking a rest." I ran to the room. No Mom. Looked in the bathroom. She wasn't there.

I went racing upstairs, and she was in bed just sobbing. She couldn't express what was wrong. I hurriedly took her blood pressure. It was 205 / 110! (Normal is about 120 / 80.) I immediately called Charlotte again. She recommended that we give

Mom an extra dose of her medication, which we immediately did. Dad had come upstairs; he hadn't known Mom was in distress. And Susan had come over from next door.

This was a very frightening time. I thought we were going to lose Mom. She was clutching her chest, shaking as if she were extremely cold (and her teeth were chattering!), and rubbing her forehead.

Gradually her blood pressure began to go down. I sat right by her on the bed, trying to soothe her and assure her we weren't going anywhere. She'd say things like, "I don't want that to happen again. I can't do that again." She'd weep and ask, "Why? Why I do this?"

When she was quiet for a while I'd wonder if she was all right, and she'd answer, "I'm meditating." The humor was there even during a crisis. I was certain she was beginning to feel better when she started making fun of me for laughing at her when she had called. She said that here she had called me with her last breath—her dying breath—and I had *laughed!*

Eventually her blood pressure went down to about 160 / 80, which was much better than it had been. And Mom began to talk, mostly about her childhood. I loved such times, hearing her tell of her love for the ocean (she lived in Fullerton, California, for much of her growing-up time) and the fun she had with cousins and neighbors.

She always had a funny story to share. One cousin had the nickname of "Spud." One day when he was playing in the ocean, he got in trouble with the undertow, and one of his friends had to rescue him. In the paper there was a slight mistake with the word *friend*, and the article said, "He rescued his fried Spud from the ocean." Such memories would bring forth Mom's wonderful, infectious laugh.

The following Monday morning, after this very frightening experience, I was at the MTC and answered the phone. I heard some unusual croaking and groaning, and I didn't know what to think. Then I heard Mom laughing, and I burst out laughing too (partly from relief!). She said, "I teach you lesson!" I'll say! She did that to me a few times, and Charlotte finally told her she should be careful about "crying wolf."

One Tuesday morning the phone rang about 5:00. It was Mom, and I could tell she was very upset. She said she'd been awake and up since 3:30.

She went on, "I got zapped." She was once again feeling the terrible sensations in her chest and head. She said she'd been trying to watch TV and wait for Dad to get up about 6:00 A.M. We talked a long time, and she said she felt better.

I left to go to work, but I hadn't gone more than a couple of miles when I had a strong—overwhelming, really—impression to go see Mom. She seemed so happy when she saw me walk through the door. In my journal I described the look on her face as one that said, "I *knew* you'd come!" I felt so grateful I had responded to this prompting by the Spirit.

There she was, sitting in the living room alone, covered with a blanket, waiting for Dad to get up so she'd have some company. We talked for a long time about all kinds of things. There had been a storm (with thunder and lightning) the night before, and she talked about how it had frightened her.

At one point, as I got ready to leave when Dad was up, she looked at me and with emotion said, "What would I do without you?" And I felt like that was a moment—an hour—I wouldn't have traded for anything.

Once I wrote in my journal, "I'm sure there have been millions of children who have gone through this with their parents, and this is my turn, and it's *hard*." It *was* hard. Sometimes I'd have vivid dreams that Mom had died, and I'd feel so horrible. Often I'd feel helpless, not knowing what to do or say. But I have to say that Mom's incredible sense of humor and her cheerful optimism made all the difference.

There were quite a few trips to visit physicians during the

first few weeks and months after the stroke. Mom was unpredictable with her keen sense of humor. Once when a nurse at an office was taking her blood pressure and couldn't quite hear it, she warned Mom, "You can't talk," and Charlotte and I answered, "You're right!" We all got laughing so hard that it was a while before the nurse could get the blood-pressure reading.

Another time when the nurse couldn't seem to hear or get Mom's blood pressure, Mom remarked, "I was alive just a few minutes ago."

In the hospital, when the lab person would call her name to have her come in and get her blood drawn, I loved saying things like, "Be brave, Mom. Try not to scream or faint." And she'd always do something hilarious to go along with what I'd said, cheering up others who were waiting.

On a Sunday late in April, Mom had a memorable experience on a very difficult day. She had planned to go to sacrament meeting, but then began to feel sick. She had the same tight feelings in her chest and head.

She said she talked to Heavenly Father about it, wondering if this was her way, even unconsciously, of getting out of going to church. But she kept feeling worse, so she went to bed. Dad had given her a blessing before she went to lie down, but even so she began to feel frightened and desperate.

She later told us that she'd felt like she was dying. She said, "It was probably a dream, but I can still see it so clearly." Something had happened in her head. She said it was a feeling and sound like shattering glass. And then she was out of her body and felt extremely peaceful and free.

She said she thought, "So here it is. Now I'm dying." And her first thought was, "Mary Ellen—what will she do?" She explained that she thought that because she had told me she would rather die than have another stroke. I told her I remembered and understood.

Then she said she thought of her family, "What will they do?" She said next she felt the sun coming through the window of the bedroom, and she opened her eyes and realized she was still here. It was so sweet and tender listening to her try to tell us what she had experienced.

As I worked on this particular chapter for the book, Mom was aware of what I was doing. One day when I told her I was almost finished, she sat thinking about it and then said, "Tell them at first it was funny; now it's not funny anymore." And then she burst out laughing, and so did I. She has the uncanny ability to share something with a serious approach and then end up laughing about it.

Soon after Mom's stroke, I knew there was one thing she would think of sooner or later. She had been invited to participate in the women's conference at BYU in April of that year, 1993. I felt she would probably decide she couldn't do it, but I told her I thought she would have a powerful, meaningful message for the women.

I was thinking the upcoming talk would give Mom a goal that would help her in some very specific ways, even though I was concerned that it not be too much pressure. I told her we'd all help her in any way we could to get ready.

The person in charge of the women's conference, Carol Lee Hawkins, came to visit Mom in the hospital. She came to assure her that she was still on, telling her, "You're my only farmer! You *have* to be there!" I pay tribute to Carol Lee for knowing what it would mean to Mom to participate in such an event—and even what it would mean to work to get ready!

Mom worked hard. She had been asked to talk about the seasons in her life, and everyone was already feeling how powerful it would be to have her tell about this particular experience and season.

And so, as time went on, we began to work on her talk. She'd share thoughts, and I'd write as fast as I could. She told me several times that when she was lying in bed at night and in the early morning she'd get *fantastic* ideas, but she couldn't write them down. But sometimes she'd try to write notes on pieces of paper and the backs of envelopes (those are her "planners"), and I could usually tell what she had tried to write.

When Mom would have her bad days, I'd ask her if it was because of any stress or pressure she might be feeling in connection with the women's conference. She would always answer "no." Once she was very emphatic. "No! I *want* to do that—I have expertise!" When a big and complicated word like that would come out, we'd get so excited!

As we came up with several drafts of what Mom wanted to share, we realized that she wouldn't be able to get through it alone. She asked Charlotte to help her. Once when we were practicing, she said that during the talk, "I can turn to her and say 'Oh, Charlotte, I'm feeling too much pressure—it's your turn—I don't need another stroke,'" and then she laughed and laughed. What a good sport.

A few days before the conference, we were practicing with the slides we were going to use to illustrate the talk. We had felt the need to give more of the reading to Charlotte, and Mom was cheerful about doing so. Once Charlotte was kind of stuttering over a word or two, and Mom said, "Who had the stroke?"

Finally it was Thursday, April 29, 1993. The time had come. And it was one of Mom's finest hours.

I called Mom early in the morning and started with, "Hi. Anything happening today?" She laughed and said, "Oh, no. I think I will rest today and hear Paul's talk tomorrow" (my brother Paul was giving a talk at the same conference on Friday).

Many family members and friends came for the event, wanting to support Mom in this important milestone in her efforts to come back from the stroke. I loved watching Dad in the audience with us, waving his white cap her direction to let her know he was with her and wished her well.

It was magical and spectacular. Mom even added some spontaneous things, which gave us the indication that she was relaxed and enjoying herself even with her limitations. She and Charlotte got a standing ovation! And people swarmed around Mom afterward, telling her how well she had done.

I'd like to close this chapter with some excerpts from her presentation, because I think there's no better illustration of how a merry heart and a sense of humor can help a person be truly happy even in times of great adversity. She read part of it, and Charlotte read part, but the words were all Mom's:

> I was asked to participate in this panel last year. Then, on the first Sunday of the New Year, January 3rd, I had a stroke, and in a way that has changed everything.
>
> I had this stroke on purpose, knowing I'd be making a presentation at this women's conference—I wanted to have a new, different perspective.
>
> I have thought for a long time about what I want to share. What I know best is *me*.

Mom went on to share some thoughts about her growing up in California and her education and marriage. And then she said:

> We have had a busy, full life, full of activity in the Church and community as well as in the family. It has included Scouting, girls' camp, road shows, Relief Society bazaars (they're extinct now), and so much more.
>
> We have come to love the land, but hope there won't be rocks in heaven. We have come to love our animals, and we look forward to seeing all of them again on the "Other Side." And surely if we do farming there, we won't have any midnight water turns! Sometimes as we look back we think of the many choices we've had to make and realize that we have always done what we felt was best in raising our

children—teaching them the work ethic and other gospel principles.

When I think of composing, and of our fifty-six years, I think of notes. We've had some C's, some A's, some F sharps, and quite a few B flats and sour notes. And then came Sunday, January 3rd, 1993.

It seemed like all at once the many notes I'd been composing for seventy-eight years got scattered. This season of my life seems like "The Lost Chord." The notes have been scrambled, and I'm trying to get them back in the right order.

I knew everything, even if no one else did! My thoughts have always been clear. I have had so many feelings inside, and no way to express them.

One word came back quickly. It's a four-letter word and it starts with "H" and ends with "L" but I can't say it today in this place. I've had to start over, line by line, word by word.

When I had the stroke and I couldn't talk or anything, everyone had a story: "Aunt so-and-so was in *exactly* the same condition." "Oh, I know *just* what you're going through—my mother . . ." "My friend had the *very same thing* happen to her—I know *exactly* how you feel."

I'm ME!! This is my very own experience, separate and different from what has happened to anyone else. I'm unique—I'm *not* exactly like anyone else. And I don't want people to think my mind's gone!

I lost my "Three R's," after all these years. I think if you're going to have a stroke, you should have it when you're younger. You see, the trouble is, I waited too long to have my stroke. I'd have enjoyed it a lot more if I'd been younger. I'd have recovered faster. So if you're thinking of having a stroke, don't wait too long!

Sometimes I've been in the depths of despair, and other times I've been ecstatic with happiness. In my lonely hours, especially for the first hours and days after I had the stroke, I wasn't exactly frightened . . . but I sure did a lot of praying inside. I do have and have had some dark hours in this mind of mine. I have anguish and loneliness and sometimes I'm despondent.

But I'm generally a very positive, happy person. I believe in having a positive mental attitude, and I've laughed a lot in life. . . . I don't want sad things or pessimism around me.

Inside, my feelings seem more tender—I notice music and things I read differently, and they touch me. I came to realize that I wouldn't have minded if I had died. I felt ready and peaceful. So many things have changed.

I realize that in this season of my composing of my life, my strength isn't in writing a poem or painting a picture. I don't *have* a poem I've written or a picture I've painted. And they wouldn't let me bring my five donkeys to show you.

I have never really aspired to be in the limelight. I recognize that if everyone were a star, who would do the clapping? I *love* to clap! And I can *do* that!

I've had my chances to be in front—to teach the Scouts and do the road shows, to go to girls' camp and milk the cows, to raise my children and care for my animals—and now I have my many memories.

When I think of composing, I think that sometimes a whole orchestra is too much. Sometimes a single note, like the train whistle, is very soothing and comforting.

Composing my life is still a work in progress. Life is full and good, and I'm so glad to be me—MYSELF! In the name of Jesus Christ, Amen.

Chapter 10

O REMEMBER,
REMEMBER

HAVE YOU EVER NOTICED HOW often the word *remember* is used in the scriptures, especially in the Book of Mormon? It seems that the Lord has to keep reminding us to remember how kind and helpful He has been to His children through all the generations.

Simply put, *remembering* tends to bring happiness. It's a word that calls to mind the blessings of perspective and awareness. Of course, there are some things in life that are painful to remember, but for the purposes of this discussion let's assume that we're talking about the healing kind of remembering mentioned in the scriptures.

Sometimes our stress and discouragement, our unhappiness, our feelings of burnout and hopelessness, are a result of forgetting. We forget how much Heavenly Father has helped us in the past, and we forget how much He wants to help us now and in the future. We forget to ask for His help. We forget how much He has promised to those who knock, seek, and ask.

Remembering is tied to gratitude and contentment. When we forget about our abundance of blessings, we tend to become unhappy. Forgetting can bring feelings of impatience, selfishness, and greed. Remembering, on the other hand, helps us feel happy in our abundance and more responsive to promptings to share it.

I'd like everyone to participate in an activity (did I think to mention that this would be a workbook?) to help illustrate what I mean. Let's start this way: Can you think of some reasons you have in your life to be happy, grateful, content, and at peace? Part of this exercise may help you remember some things for which you haven't expressed thanks in a long, long time. It's meant to help push thoughts toward gratitude and happiness.

So here's what I'm going to do. I'm going to give twenty-five true-or-false-type statements. As you read, please keep track of how many of the twenty-five bring an honest "yes" to your mind.

In the beginning, as you start responding to these twenty-five things, you may wonder what in the world I'm getting at. Hang in there.

Here's a sample, just to get you started:

00. *I'd rather be sleeping right now.*

If your answer is "yes," you get one point. Got it? Now try all twenty-five and let's see what happens. (And "00" is not one of the twenty-five, so don't think for a *single minute* that you're going to start with a point already.)

01. I have electricity in the place where I live.

02. I have noticed something beautiful in the weather or scenery today.

03. I am a child of God.

04. I will have enough food to eat today.

05. I have forgiven someone of something within the past year, even though it was difficult for me to do.

06. I can read.

07. I voted for the great plan of happiness.

08. Within the past twenty-four hours, I have laughed—really laughed.

09. I can think of at least ten people who know me very well and love me very much.

10. I have witnessed a miracle within the past year.

11. I live within a few hours of a temple.

12. I have a bed.

13. I know how to find at least one constellation among the stars.

14. There are at least ten things I enjoy at this time in my life that hadn't yet been discovered or invented when I was born.

15. I have communicated with my Heavenly Father in a meaningful way within the past twenty-four hours.

16. There is something I'm looking forward to.

17. I can think of at least five traditions in my family that are enjoyable, meaningful, and important to me.

18. I don't usually have to boil the water I drink.

19. I can remember offering a prayer in which I only thanked Heavenly Father, and I didn't ask for anything.

20. I have said or done something nice for someone within the past week.

21. I've done something recently that I've been meaning to do for quite a while.

22. There's at least one thing I'm good at—one thing I can do well.

23. Within the past week, I have had a wonderful experience while reading from the scriptures.

24. I have been forgiven of something that previously was weighing heavily on my mind.

25. Jesus Christ is my Savior, my Redeemer, my Light, my Advocate with the Father.

How did it go? Did you keep track of how many you were able to say "yes" to? I'm wondering if anyone got all twenty-five. If so, I say WOW to you!

It's my deep feeling that if we're able to respond "yes" to at least twenty of these statements, we are on the verge of Big Happiness! We have a whole bunch of reasons to be happy, content, peaceful, generous, and optimistic!

Isn't life good? Aren't we blessed? As we count our many blessings and name them one by one, it will surprise us what the Lord has done. It will surprise us over and over and over again. Most of us could quickly make a list of a hundred things and more for which we're very thankful.

I'd like to go back through those twenty-five statements and make a few comments. You've likely thought of many responses of your own, so they're much more meaningful for you personally than anything I could add. But you know I'll comment anyway. I can't resist!

As we go back through the twenty-five, I want to share why it seems that happiness has so much to do with remembering—with awareness and perspective.

01. I have electricity in the place where I live.

Perhaps you read the first statement and thought, "Huh? Of course I have electricity in the place where I live!"

But think about it. Have you ever been without electricity? Do you have any idea how many people in our world live without it all the time?

Think of a time when your electric power has been temporarily cut off. I've heard from time to time of terrible storms, like ice storms or hurricanes or tornadoes, that have left people without electricity for days or even weeks. If that has happened to you, what did you learn? How did it feel?

Maybe you've just had the power go off for a few seconds or a few minutes, but how many appliances did you have to reset? The clocks, the radios, the TV and VCR? The microwave, the sprinkling and alarm systems?

Isn't electricity a miracle? Aren't we blessed and lucky to have such an amazing resource surrounding us? Isn't it remarkable that there are so few times when most of us must get along without it? O remember!

02. I have noticed something beautiful in the weather or scenery today.

Some have expressed this with the little thought, "Stop and smell the roses." Do you ever catch yourself complaining that it's too hot in the summer and too cold in the winter? Are there too few times when you feel genuinely grateful for a day just the way it is? Maybe we should more often do what we may have learned to sing as little children: Stop, look, and listen!

Can you remember the last time you thanked Heavenly Father for something beautiful He has created and shared with us? Think of how much love He has expressed for us in surrounding us with such interesting and magnificent creations.

03. I am a child of God.

Imagine the *wonder* of this—knowing our relationship to our Heavenly Father! I'm convinced that such knowledge changes everything and brings with it a sense of belonging and worth.

It's when we forget or doubt this relationship that we feel estranged from Him. When we imagine our Heavenly Father mad or simply continually disappointed in us, the distance between us seems to grow. *He* doesn't move. He doesn't quit loving us and caring about us. He never will cease to yearn for us to come close to Him, to talk to Him, to worship Him, to remember Him.

04. I will have enough food to eat today.

Can you comprehend the idea of millions of people in the world who have never felt full? When we remember that many of Heavenly Father's children go through life hungry and thirsty (and perhaps naked and sick) almost constantly, it should bring into our hearts a great, deep sense of appreciation that we are so abundantly blessed with more than we need.

I've even thought of such things in relation to fasting. When I fast, I often "line up" (in my mind, if not literally) the things I'm going to eat and drink as the second hand comes around to twenty-four hours. The majority of people in this world "fast" (at least they go without food) because there is nothing to eat or drink. It's not a choice, it's a reality.

I've thought about whether I eat to live or live to eat. I think there are times when I get carried away somewhat with wanting to have things look or taste a certain way. I waste too much. I eat too much. I've told quite a few people that anyone can tell I'm from Utah because I have a shape like a beehive!

Part of this food question has to do with water. I wonder how many people in the world are able to drink all they want whenever they feel thirsty. Are you able to do that most of the time? Have you ever been on a hike with just a small canteen, and you felt so thirsty, but you took small swallows and sips so the water would last? Can you imagine having it be that way almost every day of your life?

Are you like me and maybe haven't thanked Heavenly Father for food and water in a while? One thing that happens inside of me when I do remember to thank Him is an increasing desire to be careful—not to waste so much. If I'm careful, maybe He can share the food and water I didn't waste with someone who's desperately hungry and thirsty.

05. *I have forgiven someone of something within the past year, even though it was difficult for me to do.*

For this one, the "something" you forgave doesn't have to be a big thing. Even when grievances are small, it can be difficult to forgive. Pride can make it difficult. It takes humility and courage to seek forgiveness from others, and it takes those same things to offer forgiveness.

For most of us, this experience of giving the gift of forgiveness brings a remembering of how often *we* have been forgiven of our many mistakes, and of how constantly kind and merciful God is to us.

06. I can read.

Isn't this a blessing! Can you remember when you couldn't read? Has it been so long that you can't remember the joy and excitement of beginning to learn to read—to recognize letters, to follow along when someone read to you, to sound out and figure out some of those first words on your very own?

So many of Heavenly Father's children can't read or write. What would it be like? How would it feel not to be able to read the Book of Mormon or any other scriptures, or the words of the hymns, or the lessons for Church meetings, or the *Ensign* (especially the one with the conference reports), or the newspaper, or . . . well, we could go on and on, couldn't we.

What would it be like for a parent not to be able to write to a son or daughter on a mission, or read a letter written back? I think it would be a powerful reminder (and that word has got to be at least a cousin to *remember*) if we kept track of how many times during even one day we need to be able to read and write in order to carry on.

07. I voted for the great plan of happiness.

Remembering that we kept our first estate ought to keep us pondering and expressing thanks for the rest of forever. We had understanding, we exercised agency, we chose, and we shouted for joy! Why, then, do we forget this and spend so much of our time being grumpy and crabby?

08. Within the past twenty-four hours, I have laughed—really laughed.

I'm talking about happy laughter, the "good kind." The kind that comes from the heart and from a genuine feeling of happiness. The kind that feels good (and returns) long after the moment of happification.

09. I can think of at least ten people who know me very well and love me very much.

Those on your list don't have to be in your own home or neighborhood or even in your own community or nation. They don't even have to be alive! Well, I just mean that they could be on the Other Side—in heaven.

I put in the phrase "know me very well" because it seems the better we understand someone, the better we know the person's heart, the more our love is genuine and the longer it lasts. It lasts through the times when we may not be pleasant or obedient, when we may not return the love shown to us (let alone be the first to express it), and when we may try to run and hide.

So can you think of ten people who know you that well and love you that much? Be sure to list your Heavenly Father and the Savior. Now you just have to think of eight more. I know you can do it. I wish I could be sitting beside you to prompt you if you're having trouble coming up with ten. I wish you could open your memory—that you could remember those who do love you, no matter where they are right now.

10. I have witnessed a miracle within the past year.

Many times when we think of miracles we think of the BIG kind. Have we forgotten the last time we held a new little baby? Have we forgotten the sound of the ocean or the view from the top of the hill?

Can you remember the first time you used a telephone or a computer? Have these ceased being miracles? How about a microwave oven or a jet taking off? Can you remember the awe you've felt watching a sunrise or a sunset, and the view of the earth radioed down from an orbiting shuttle?

How about the colors on flowers and lizards, or the tiny things surviving in a desert, or the shells in the sand at the beach? Have you witnessed a miracle within the past year? You've witnessed it within the last minute, haven't you, just in realizing that your heart is beating, your lungs are taking in and helping distribute oxygen, your eyes are looking at these words, and your brain is understanding them. There are miracles all around us all the time.

11. I live within a few hours of a temple.

Some who read this will wonder if I mean within a few hours if they walk or drive or fly or go by boat or . . . My answer is yes.

It's good I didn't try to write this statement even ten years ago, or the answers would be much different. Perhaps I could ask that you respond based on what *is*, but also based on what *will be*. Has there been an announcement about a temple to be built even closer to you than the one you now can reach with some sacrifice and difficulty?

I feel so thankful that there are so many more temples being built. Remember when we used to have to name all the temples as we graduated from Primary? I had to name *all eight!* If we had to do that now, I guess I'd never get out of Primary! I also remember when there were some members of the Church who could say they had visited every single temple. Likely there are a few who could do that now (would they be mostly General Authorities?), but most of us can't even remember where they *are!* Fantastic!

One early morning I was headed to Salt Lake for some meetings, and I left early so I'd have time to go to the Salt Lake Temple. As I was driving along, thinking about "whatever," the still small voice came into my mind. "Edmunds, are you ready to go to the temple today?" Almost instantly, without thinking much at all, I responded, "Yup. I've got my recommend and my clothing—I'm ready."

Then I felt an impression like, "That's not what I meant." "Ohhhhh . . . what did you mean?" "Are you *ready?*" And then I was reminded—I remembered—that there were probably many others going to the temple that same day who were ready in ways that I wasn't. What if it was their first time? What if they'd been waiting for years? What if it was going to be their only time (so far as they could tell on this particular morning)?

And so I spent the rest of the trip to Salt Lake thinking and feeling deeply about how much I wanted to be as ready as I knew others were and would be. I wanted so much to feel something of what *they* were feeling. I wanted not just to be worthy—although I knew that was critical—but to be ready in the way I was taught.

When I visit people in other places, I'm always interested in knowing where "their" temple is. I happened to make several trips to Nashville, Tennessee, at a time when they'd been waiting a few years to try to get permission to build the temple that had been announced for their area. They had some beautiful property, which I got to see.

But then in court a decision went against them. I felt so sad about that. The next time I went there, I talked to some of the Church leaders about it, and I was stunned and deeply moved by their response. They weren't "ticked off" or frustrated. Maybe they had been for a little while, but at this point they were humble instead. One of them said to me, "We're working hard to be worthy of a temple. When we're ready, God will give us our temple."

And now there has been an announcement about another location and likely a smaller temple, and they are thrilled. I am too. I'm happy they're going to get their temple, and I'm happy for what they helped me learn and feel.

A few years ago I was in Louisiana. As usual, I asked where the closest temple was. "Dallas," was the answer. I wondered how long it took them to get there. "Ten hours—twenty hours round-trip." Wow. But then they added with great enthusiasm, "But soon there'll be a temple in Houston, and then it will only take us six hours to get there!"

And inside myself I was thinking that in six hours I could get to probably thirteen or fourteen temples from where I live.

Do I remember what a blessing it is to be able to go to the House of the Lord and worship, learn, feel peace, and all else that comes with this privilege?

By the way, now I've heard there's going to be a temple in Baton Rouge!

12. I have a bed.

At first I wanted this one to say, "I have a home." Instead I wrote it this way. I have wondered if some would read it and say, "Well, it's only a mat on a floor," or "It's not very fancy," or "Most people have beds that are a lot bigger, newer, and more comfortable than mine." But all I wrote was: I have a bed. I needed to say it that way for *me*, because sometimes when I get in my bed I think about how long I've had the mattress (since 1970) and focus on that instead of being thankful to have a bed.

I have hoped the statement "I have a bed" would also be a reminder that many of us have a place to put our heads—a place where we can go and *belong*. Hopefully for most of us it is a refuge and a safe place, with others nearby who love and care for us. May we not forget what a blessing it is to have a bed.

13. I know how to find at least one constellation among the stars.

Have we looked up into the heavens enough? Have we thought of the expanse that's above and all around us? Have we considered our insignificance, while at the same time knowing that the Creator of all we can see and all we can't see is aware of us in a very personal and specific way?

Don't ignore the stars. Don't forget to look at them and think about them occasionally. Remember that God is in His heaven, and every star is numbered, and every child (that's us!) is known and loved.

14. There are at least ten things I enjoy at this time in my life that hadn't yet been discovered or invented when I was born.

This will be easier for some of us than for others. I used to love asking my dad about things he'd seen over the course of his life. He was born in 1902 and lived ninety-five years! He had seen almost a century of discovery and progress—and oh, what a century!

One of my favorite stories was when he'd tell us about the man who got the first automobile in Wales, Utah, the little community where my father was born. Dad would tell us of the man chugging slowly into the shed where he was going to keep the car, and going right through the other side (destroying the shed), shouting, "Whoa! Whoa!"

What are some of the things you enjoy, things that make your life more pleasant and even easier? Electricity? Some who read this book will remember living without it for at least part of their lives. Running water? Indoor plumbing? How about heating and air conditioning (for homes *and* cars)? We could list so many things: computers, zip-lock bags, penicillin, WD-40, jets, satellites, Velcro, TV, batteries, disposable diapers, frozen foods, bread-making machines, mechanical pencils, answering machines, call waiting, cruise control, duct tape . . .

Isn't it incredible to remember even a few of the things that make our lives so full and interesting? How blessed we are!

15. I have communicated with my Heavenly Father in a meaningful way within the past twenty-four hours.

At first I was going to have this statement read, "I have prayed within the last twenty-four hours." Then I remembered that many of my prayers are not very meaningful. I'd have to say that there are times when my prayers might be termed "boring." Ouch. Communicating with our Heavenly Father in a meaningful way is what prayer ought to be.

I love how the *Bible Dictionary* explains prayer. I'll include just a short excerpt so you can see what I mean:

> As soon as we learn the true relationship in which we stand toward God (namely, God is our Father, and we are his children), then at once prayer becomes natural and instinctive on our part (Matt. 7:7–11). Many of the

179

so-called difficulties about prayer arise from forgetting [aha!] this relationship. Prayer is the act by which the will of the Father and the will of the child are brought into correspondence with each other. The object of prayer is not to change the will of God, but to secure for ourselves and for others blessings that God is already willing to grant, but that are made conditional on our asking for them. Blessings require some work or effort on our part before we can obtain them. Prayer is a form of work, and is an appointed means for obtaining the highest of all blessings. (*Bible Dictionary*, pp. 752–53)

Isn't that powerful? God loves to hear from us. He's our Father. He wants to know what we're thinking and feeling. He asks us to share our innermost thoughts with Him so that *we* can understand better what we're thinking and feeling. He already has blessings He's willing to share with us, but they've been made conditional on our asking for them. Oh, this is beautiful and important! Remember to make your communication with your Heavenly Father real and meaningful. Let it become the blessing and privilege it is meant to be.

16. There is something I'm looking forward to.

Anticipation is a great source of happiness. Remembering that something good is going to happen can lift our spirits and chase away the dark clouds almost any day. I guess there's nothing more spectacular or motivating to look forward to than a time when we can return Home to our Heavenly Parents kind and dear, and see our loved ones who are there now and who wait for us with great love and tenderness. I hope you were able to think of at least one thing you're looking forward to!

17. I can think of at least five traditions in my family that are enjoyable, meaningful, and important to me.

What are your family traditions? The way you remember Christ at Christmas? The one-on-one time with parents? The hundreds of Monday evenings with the family? The annual trip to visit relatives in another place? Sunday dinner with happy laughter as memories are once again shared? Sparklers on the Fourth of July, or other ways of celebrating important holidays in your place? The parades where you'd decorate your bicycle tires or haul your bunny down Main Street in a wagon? What are the traditions that bring sweet, nostalgic memories to your mind?

18. I don't usually have to boil the water I drink.

I included the word *usually* here because I know there are people out there who help with Scout and Young Women camps, and people who live in places where the water is sometimes contaminated (like with a dead raccoon or a broken pipe or something). But imagine—there are millions of people who don't *ever* have water that doesn't need to be boiled or purified in some other way! Remember when you take a long drink of cool water at a time when you're very thirsty that it's a great, good blessing.

Remember, too, that there's another kind of water about which Jesus taught, and when we drink of that water we are promised we will never thirst again! We can share both kinds of water with others. Let's not forget to do that.

19. I can remember offering a prayer in which I only thanked Heavenly Father, and I didn't ask for anything.

One of my friends said her stake president invited everyone to find time for a long prayer, and in that prayer they would thank their Heavenly Father for everything they could think of for which they were thankful. Everything. They would be specific. They would "name them one by one."

Then he asked them to have this on their minds for the rest of the day and even longer, and when they remembered something they'd forgotten to include, they would think of what their lives would be like without that particular blessing. What a lesson in gratitude this can be! What a powerful reminder!

Elder Henry B. Eyring taught this in a beautiful way:

You could have an experience with the gift of the Holy Ghost today. You could begin a private prayer with thanks. You could start to count your blessings, and then pause for a moment. If you exercise faith, and with the gift of the Holy Ghost, you will find that memories of other blessings will flood into your mind. If you begin to express gratitude for each of them, your prayer may take a little longer than usual. Remembrance will come. And so will gratitude. (*Ensign*, November 1989, p. 13)

20. I have said or done something nice for someone within the past week.

Of course you have. Did you thank someone who helped you choose a watermelon at the grocery store? Did you compliment a teacher on the lesson given last week? Did you motion for another driver to go ahead of you? Did you give away smiles? Did you pick up a pencil someone had dropped? Did you thank a classmate for taking notes for you when you were sick? Did you call and wish someone a happy birthday? Did you get a surprise treat for a member of your family?

It seems to me that people forget their kindnesses. Sometimes they think what they do isn't worth much, or they're not making a difference for anyone, or they're far, far away from being Christlike in their behavior.

I believe you're not as far away as you might think sometimes at points of discouragement or exhaustion. Remember that you've been kind and nice to others, and *know* that you're doing many good things!

21. I've done something recently that I've been meaning to do for quite a while.

I tried to give the reader a lot of flexibility here. "Recently" could mean in the past week, but it could also mean within the past year. (That's "recent" if you're over thirty or even twenty!) And "quite a while" could mean a month, a year, or a decade or more. So almost everyone should be able to answer "yes" to this one.

What did you get done? Did you get your "junk room" cleaned out? Did you start exercising regularly? Have you figured out a way, time, and place to make your scripture study more enjoyable? Did you take a class or a trip? Did you write a poem or a story? Did you get through *Les Misérables?* Did you invite neighbors over for family home evening? Did you make a phone call? Did you get the pine tree planted? Did you think to pray? (Ha—just wanted to see if you were paying attention.)

Doesn't it feel good to get something done you've been meaning to do—a letter or a visit or a project or whatever? For me it's a reminder of how good life is, and how nice it is to have promptings come into our minds and hearts, reminding us of things we've been meaning to do. Is it time?

22. There's at least one thing I'm good at—one thing I can do well.

I feel strongly about this one as a reminder to us that every child of God has been given gifts. Some have quite a few! But we all have some gifts and talents. What are yours? What is one thing you're good at?

It might be quilting or cabinet making, singing or sailing, giving or receiving. Maybe you have the gift of compassion, or of being an effective teacher or learner. Perhaps you're good at cheering others up or fixing wonderful meals. (That would cheer *me* up!) Is your gift to have great faith in Jesus Christ?

Moroni reminds us that "all these gifts come by the Spirit of Christ; and they come unto every man severally, according as he will. And I would exhort you, my beloved brethren, that ye remember [there's that word again] that every good gift cometh of Christ" (Moroni 10:17–18).

23. Within the past week, I have had a wonderful experience while reading from the scriptures.

What have you learned in your life about how to make scripture study a meaningful part of your days? Likely it's not the number of pages or the amount of time only—am I right?

How do you invite the Spirit to teach you as you search? And what does the word *search* mean that is different from *read*? Does it help when you pray first? Does it help if you write down some of your feelings? Does it help if you put your own name into some of the verses of instruction, comfort, and so on?

The scriptures are *filled* with *remember*. Remember that you can depend on God. You can trust your Heavenly Father and the Savior and the Holy Ghost. They will help you not just to understand the scriptures but to use what you understand to make happifying changes in your life. Even if every single experience isn't a "whopper," as you'd like it to be, please don't stop coming to the feast daily.

24. *I have been forgiven of something that previously was weighing heavily on my mind.*

This doesn't have to have happened within the past year or within any specified period. At *any* time in your life, have you experienced this miracle of forgiveness? I hope so. Most of us don't live perfectly, and thus we have things for which we must seek our Heavenly Father's forgiveness. And oh, what a sweet feeling there is when these particular burdens are lifted! I think you know what I mean.

"Cast thy burden upon the Lord, and he shall sustain thee" (Psalm 55:22). Christ has invited and encouraged us to give Him our burdens, to come unto Him so He can give us rest. He says His yoke is easy and His burden light (see Matthew 11:28–30). Thank goodness! What if we were trapped by all the things we've done wrong! What if there were no way to change!

25. *Jesus Christ is my Savior, my Redeemer, my Light, my Advocate with the Father.*

There it is. Number 25. The last one. The one that makes the biggest difference in our lives. To come to an assurance that this is true is one of the best and sweetest of all feelings we can have in our hearts. Remember that He stands at the door knocking, hoping we'll open our heart to Him and allow Him and His influence to come in. Oh, if we could just trust Him completely! If only we could have even a little bit more understanding of what He went through for us!

I will remember forever the day a group of us sat in the restored historic Joseph Smith Sr. home and listened to a wonderful sister missionary tell us, with emotion, that she knew that even if she'd been the only person on earth, Jesus still would have come. He still would have made the Atonement a reality. Her words reminded me that He did come just for me, and just for you.

I could have gone beyond those twenty-five statements, of course. I wanted one about the Sabbath, thinking of how the commandment is worded: "Remember the sabbath day, to keep it holy" (Exodus 20:8). I've thought a lot about how *remembering* the Sabbath day would help me to keep it holy. He could have just said, "Keep the Sabbath day holy," but He didn't.

I wanted something in the statements about living the law of the fast, tied as that is to happiness and remembering. I feel embarrassed about how many times I've looked upon fasting almost as a "near-death" experience, missing so much of the joy and rejoicing, the remembering of how God has blessed me.

I wanted something about families, especially after reading and rereading and thinking about "The Family: A Proclamation to the World."

I did have a wonderful time going through all the Standard Works, looking for phrases like "thou shalt remember" and "beware that thou forget not." Following are just a few of my favorites.

In the Old Testament, the Lord reminds the Israelites again and again what He has done for them. Here's just one injunction: " . . . that thou mayest remember the day when thou camest forth out of the land of Egypt all the days of thy life" (Deuteronomy 16:3). The Lord gives His people many ways to remember His influence in their lives.

In the Book of Mormon, forgetting seems to be tied to hardness of heart. For example, when Laman and Lemuel murmured because they did not understand their father's vision, Nephi chastised them: "How is it that ye do not keep the commandments of the Lord? How is it that ye will perish, because of the hardness of your hearts? Do ye not remember the things which the Lord hath said?—If ye will not harden your hearts, and ask me in faith, believing that ye shall receive, with diligence in keeping my commandments, surely these things shall be made known unto you" (1 Nephi 15:10–11).

It seems that Laman and Lemuel kept forgetting—that they'd seen an angel, for example. Their hard hearts were symptomatic of their forgetting, or perhaps they forgot because their hearts were hard. Soft hearts *remember*. Soft hearts are aware and grateful.

Many times in the scriptures the word *remember* is tied to action, such as in 2 Nephi 1:12, where Lehi exhorts his sons to "remember; yea, I would that ye would hearken unto my words." Remember and hearken.

Later Lehi teaches, "And I desire that ye should remember to observe the statutes and the judgments of the Lord; behold, this hath been the anxiety of my soul from the beginning" (2 Nephi 1:16). Remember and observe—*do*.

And how I love Mosiah 2:41, where King Benjamin teaches about endless happiness and closes with "O remember, remember that these things are true!"

We have been given a significant way to remember the Savior and our covenants to become like Him. Jesus taught, concerning the ordinance of the sacrament, "And this shall ye do in remembrance of my body, which I have shown unto you. And it shall be a testimony unto the Father that ye do always remember me. And if ye do always remember me ye shall have my Spirit to be with you" (3 Nephi 18:7).

Thus, as we partake of the sacrament, we hear these words: "O God, the Eternal Father, we ask thee in the name of thy Son, Jesus Christ, to bless and sanctify this bread to the souls of all those who partake of it; that they may eat in remembrance of the body of thy Son, and witness unto thee, O God, the Eternal Father, that they are willing to take upon them the name of thy Son, and always remember him, and keep his commandments which he hath given them, that they may always have his Spirit to be with them. Amen" (Moroni 4:3). And we are also instructed to remember His blood, which He shed for us (see 3 Nephi 18:11; Moroni 5:2).

Remembering the Savior often translates into remembering and caring for each other:

> And none were received unto baptism save they took upon them the name of Christ, having a determination to serve him to the end.
>
> And after they had been received unto baptism, and were wrought upon and cleansed by the power of the Holy Ghost, they were numbered among the people of the church of Christ; and their names were taken, that they might be remembered and nourished by the good word of God, to keep them in the right way, to keep them continually watchful unto prayer, relying alone upon the merits of Christ, who was the author and the finisher of their faith.
>
> And the church did meet together oft, to fast and to pray, and to speak one with another concerning the welfare of their souls.
>
> And they did meet together oft to partake of bread and wine, in remembrance of the Lord Jesus. (Moroni 6:3–6)

I am so grateful that the gospel of Jesus Christ is a gospel of taking good care of each other. We get to be "numbered," which means we get to belong. Our names are taken so that we might be remembered and nourished by one another, and so we can help each other stay in the right way—on the straight and narrow path. We meet together often so we can fast and pray, and so we can make sure everyone's all right. And we partake of the sacrament together so that we can remember the Lord Jesus and our covenants.

But the Savior indicated that we should also remember and watch over those who have not yet chosen to be baptized. Speaking of those who wouldn't repent and be numbered among His people, He taught, "Nevertheless, ye shall not cast him out of your synagogues, or your places of worship, for unto such shall ye continue to minister; for ye know not but what they will return and repent, and come unto me with full purpose of heart, and I shall heal them; and ye shall be the means of bringing salvation unto them" (3 Nephi 18:32).

Isn't this a wonderful verse? Don't give up on anyone! Continue to minister, to care, to watch over others, even if they have not yet repented and responded fully to Christ and His Atonement. "For *ye know not* . . ." We don't, do we? We must continue to do what we can to help them come back so that Christ can heal them.

As Alma prayed concerning the apostate Zoramites: "O Lord, wilt thou grant unto us that we may have success in bringing them again unto thee in Christ. Behold, O Lord, their souls are precious, and many of them are our brethren; therefore, give unto us, O Lord, power and wisdom that we may bring these, our brethren, again unto thee" (Alma 31:34–35).

We too need the Lord's power and wisdom in all our efforts to remember, nourish, and encourage those whom God prompts us to love and serve.

God lives. He loves us. Our souls are precious to Him. He wants to bless us, and He wants us to remember Him and each other. O remember, remember!

Chapter 11

REMEMBERING PK AND LEWIE

I'VE FOCUSED A LOT IN THIS BOOK on remembering our blessings—counting them, expressing thanks for them, enjoying them, sharing them. I've also tried to emphasize the importance of remembering *people*—of nurturing and nourishing, loving without condition, and never giving up. Many of Heavenly Father's children need what we can share.

I like the way the Lord taught it through the Prophet Joseph Smith in the Doctrine and Covenants: "And remember in all things the poor and the needy, the sick and the afflicted, for he that doeth not these things, the same is not my disciple" (D&C 52:40).

When I first read that verse I thought of it in temporal or physical terms. Those who were poor and needy or sick and afflicted were usually easy to spot, and it was often obvious what they needed.

However, much suffering is spiritual. Many who are "poor and needy" may be doing well in a temporal or physical sense but are not yet blessed by the principles and ordinances available through the restored gospel of Jesus Christ.

To have a hunger and thirst for the things of God—for spiritual nourishment—is perhaps an even deeper need than that for food and water. Our responsibility to each other is great.

One of the wonderful examples in my life of this way of remembering the spiritually needy comes from the experience of my father with an old college friend. Their interaction has touched the lives of all of our family in a sweet and "forever" way.

It was in the late 1920s in Chicago. My father, Paul K. Edmunds, had gone there with his brother John. John became a lawyer, and my father became a doctor. He graduated in the class of '29 from Northwestern University's medical school.

Dad was selected to fill an internship the following year at Cook County Hospital, along with one of his classmates, Lewis I. Younger. When Lewis found out that both he and Paul would be at Cook County, he asked if he might put in a bid to room with this Utah boy. My father asked him if he smoked. "No, and neither do you—that's why I want to room with you," was the response.

And so began the wonderful friendship of PK and Lewie. Although they had been classmates since about 1926 at Northwestern, their association became much closer once they were roommates.

My father became well acquainted with Lewie's parents and family, who lived in the Chicago area. Lewie's father, also a physician, was one of the teachers at Northwestern's medical school, and my father came to appreciate and admire him very much. Lewie also became acquainted with Uncle John, Dad's older brother, who was in Chicago at the time.

But mostly Lewie and Paul became well acquainted with each other. They called each other "pal" and were as close as brothers.

Lewie recalled years later, "I thought he [PK] was extremely bright, and he was a very friendly man. He took the gospel and his work seriously. He was also devoted to the Church. He did his fasting, attended his services, and was a friend to man" (*Church News*, 29 June 1996, p. 10).

Dad was always very impressed with Lewie as well, describing him as "a clean and upright young man, no bad habits whatever. I was happy to have him as my friend and still am."

"At the time we roomed together," said Lewie, "Paul didn't actively solicit my membership [in the Church], but he made me feel very contemplative about it. I was asked to fast with him and his family a couple of times."

Eventually these two pals finished their internships and then headed different directions to continue working as general and family practitioners. Dr. Younger established his practice in Winona, Minnesota. He had planned to stay only a few years and then return to his hometown of Chicago, but he never left.

My father went first to the San Joaquin Valley in California. In 1943 he moved his little family to Cedar City, Utah, and then in 1957 he took a position with the health center at Brigham Young University, and we moved to Mapleton, Utah.

Both Lewie and Dad had married nurses, which they felt was a very smart move. (I agree!) Lewie married Edith Braun ("Brownie") in 1935, and Dad married Mom (Ella Mary Middleton) in 1937.

All through these years, the two kept closely in touch. I remember that when we'd go to visit our Uncle John and Aunt Jasmine in Chicago, we'd stop in Winona to see how Lewie and Brownie were doing. And sometimes they'd come to Utah to see us.

My father was always interested in sharing the gospel of Jesus Christ with his dear friend. He would try to make sure that Lewie visited Temple Square when he came to Utah, and Dad and Mom sent Lewie and Brownie a copy of the Book of Mormon in which they had written a personal note. Dad also sent subscriptions to the *Ensign*, copies of the *Church News*, and other articles and books.

But mostly Dad sent letters. Through all the years, he would write and encourage Lewie to consider listening to the missionaries, with the hope that he would one day embrace the gospel of Jesus Christ and become a member of the Church.

In 1991, Lewie's dear wife passed away. My father felt his friend's grief and wanted so much to comfort him. He felt the best way to do that was to help Lewie understand the plan of salvation, and he continued sharing that message with him in his letters and conversations.

In 1994, as my father anticipated his ninety-second birthday (and Lewie his ninetieth), he sensed that the two of them might not be around much longer, and he wrote a particularly strong letter to his friend.

Here are some excerpts from that letter, shared by Lewie:

5 Sep '94

Dear Lewie:

I have been remiss in writing, NOT in thinking about you daily, and you have been in my prayers daily.

Lewie, I'm really concerned about your spiritual welfare. You have over the many years known about the LDS Church and have been familiar with its teachings. . . . In fact, it was its Word of Wisdom which you were already practicing—that led you to ask to room with me at County; and we were as blood-brothers the while we were there; a . . . friendship (brotherhood) continued over the more than three score years since then.

You evidenced some interest in the Church while at County. I remember Bob . . . inviting you to spend a weekend with him in Peoria. Sun. morning (Bob told me this) he expected you to go to Mass at 6 A.M. (He thought you were Catholic like he). When you slept on, he decided you planned to go to the later Mass. When you still didn't, he asked you point-blank what church you belonged to. Your reply: "I guess I come nearer being a Mormon than anything else."

Would that you had come "all the way." It still—after 60 yrs, is still not too late. But don't wait too long! Your chance will be gone forever when you come to the end of this life. . . .

I'm sure you have a Book of Mormon. If you haven't read it, please do so. But a caveat: Read it with the purpose of mind of determining that it is true. Read it with a belief that it is true. Otherwise you may not receive Moroni's promise as recorded in Moroni 10. This bit of advice is most important—true. . . .

Well Pal, keep smiling. We love you and wish "the very best" for you—the Gospel of Jesus Christ, as revealed in the Standard Works (Bible, Book of Mormon, and Latter-day revelations as recorded in the Doctrine and Covenants from 1830 to date).

Ella & PK

After Dad sent this letter to his dear friend, he didn't hear from him for almost a month. Worried, Dad sent a follow-up note:

Out West
03 Oct '94
Dear Lewie:
Not having heard from you I fear I offended you in some way by my letter.

Know this, dear Lewie, that I prize your friendship over the many years, and that the purpose in sending you the letter—which bespoke truth—was to accomplish this friendship hereafter throughout eternity.

Please believe that it was my love for you that persuaded (urged) me to write the letter. Let us, leastwise, remain dear friends to the end of time: For me not many more years.

PK

Finally Lewie responded. In part, he wrote:

I was deeply moved by your letter today & have renewed my thinking about your concern as truly so real and a source

of pride for me to accept it. I envy your complete commit-
ment. Your faith in your beliefs makes you a very holy person.

I have no intellectual answer to you. My feeling is that I
am committed to my present course of action, incomplete
as it may be & as regrettable as I may find out in the hereafter.

You have the radiance of a saint. You're experiencing a
zeal that must make you very happy.

Please don't feel that you failed me because I in my limited religious capacities [am] failing you. Do not feel that the
outcome of my sin of omission is in any way your failure. In
order for me to change I must be changed. I must get a revelation. I will pray and try. I am willing to try. . . . I will pray
every day & read.

I can't say yes unless I am willing to go all out like you.
. . . I just haven't matured to your level of religiosity. A force
must arise within me. You are a wonderful motivating power
but I must feel it internally. I don't know why I don't have
the [assurance] that you have about the hereafter.

I am impressed that these two great pals were able to be so
honest with each other in sharing their deepest feelings. Dad
was worried he might offend Lewie, and Lewie didn't want to
disappoint Dad. Yet their bond of love and brotherhood—
their *true* friendship—tied them together in a way so deep and
lasting that they could search and share in complete honesty.

In my mind I've pictured these few weeks of their lives as a
last earthly effort to bridge the one gap that remained in their
relationship. Dad wanted their friendship to endure through
eternity, and he felt he was responsible to do all he could to
help that happen. I imagine him reaching toward his pal with
an invitation that came from the center of his soul. I imagine
Lewie reaching to grasp Dad's outstretched hand, wanting to
accept the invitation, but only if he personally understood and
could respond with all his soul.

At some point during these weeks, Lewie called Dad. Dad

told me that their conversation was honest and tender. He said that Lewie asked something like, "Paul, what would you have me do?" He had responded, "Lewie, it's time." He asked his dear friend to let the missionaries come. "Let them teach you the message. Then you carefully and prayerfully consider all they share and make your own decision, but *it's time*."

Lewie agreed! So Dad asked me to call the mission in Minnesota to tell them about this referral. I had the pleasure of talking to Elder Benton L. Blake, whom I had met when he and his wife were in the Missionary Training Center. He said there was a small branch in Winona and that they had some very fine elders serving there, and he'd let them know about Dr. Younger.

It turned out Lewie had already contacted the missionaries! I guess when he finally agreed to do what his pal PK had asked, he went right to it. Elder Blake called me back at the MTC to let me know the missionaries had an appointment with Dr. Younger.

I remember when I went home on that day in November, my parents were out in the barn doing the chores. I went out and told them I had something to tell them when they came in. They were both curious and wanted me to tell them right then, but I told them we had to be sitting down.

When they came in, we sat together at the kitchen table, and I began to cry. I couldn't help it. I told them that Lewie had an appointment to meet with the missionaries. There is no way to describe the joy of that moment, especially as I watched the emotion in my father's response.

Elders Job Bork and Daniel Boles first called on Lewie on November 9, 1994. He apparently told them he'd like to be baptized into their church because it would make his friend Paul out in Utah so happy. The elders invited him to do two things on that first visit. They asked if he would read in the Book of Mormon every day, and he said he could surely do that because he was retired and had the time, and now he had the interest. They also asked him if he would pray every day and ask his Heavenly Father if what he was reading was true—if it was from Him. He agreed to that as well.

The missionaries began to notice a change. Not only did Lewie's testimony begin to grow, but they described him as being "hungry." One of the missionaries reported, "Even his countenance is different." The missionaries said that "he made a 180-degree turn and really lit up!" They said that his eyes were literally brighter. They could tell his heart was changing.

Lewie wanted to take things slowly and surely, because, as he explained to the missionaries, he wanted to reflect and pon-der upon what he was learning. Slowly but surely, changes were happening inside of him.

And then came the phone call to let my father know that his dear pal was to be baptized the week before Christmas, and that he wanted my father to confirm him a member of the Church. (I somehow felt they were afraid to let Dad perform the actual baptism for fear he and Lewie would both drown!)

Dad wasn't sure he could make such a trip at his age and in the middle of winter, but we all felt it was critical that he be there. John, one of my younger brothers, went ahead and made all the arrangements for the two of them to fly to Minneapolis and then drive to Winona.

They went to Lewie's home shortly after they arrived on that cold Sunday in December, one week before Christmas. Dad later told me that Lewie was right there, waiting and watching for them to arrive. John said when the two friends hugged each other they almost fell over! Can you imagine what they must have been feeling!

John took some pictures as these two pals sat in Lewie's par-lor visiting. Lewie showed Dad and John the copy of the Book of Mormon that Dad and Mom had sent so many years earlier. He also showed John a stack of letters—he'd saved every single letter my dad had ever sent him! Lewie told John he had never met anyone who wrote as well as Dad. It deeply touched Dad to realize that Lewie had saved all the letters.

Later that day, Church members and friends gathered for the baptism. The elders reported that more people came to the baptismal service than usually attended the branch meetings on Sundays. None of the speakers seemed able to finish their talks. The emotions kept spilling over.

A high-backed chair was placed right by the font so that Dad could sit there and see and hear everything very well. And then Elder Bork baptized Dr. Lewis I. Younger. When he came up out of the water, Lewie reached up and grabbed Dad's hands in his. John told me that there were few if any dry eyes at that moment.

Oh, dear reader, can you imagine the sweet emotions of joy and pure happiness these two dear friends were feeling after *almost seventy years?* It is almost more than I can handle to think about it. This was the real thing. Nothing temporary or "ersatz" on this glorious December 18, 1994.

Later, PK, age ninety-two, laid his hands on the head of his friend Lewie, age ninety, and confirmed him a member of The Church of Jesus Christ of Latter-day Saints and, by the authority of the priesthood he held, invited him to receive the Holy Ghost. John said Dad gave his friend a beautiful blessing, and that his voice was strong and powerful as he shared as prompted by the Spirit.

My brother John wept as he shared all of this with me on his return from Minnesota. I did too. By the time he had finished sharing the details and showing me pictures, it was as if I'd been there too. I'm so grateful to him for his willingness to allow Dad (and Lewie) to have this unforgettably sweet moment together. I think he may not ever have given Dad a sweeter gift ever than to take him on this trip.

A letter from Lewie expressing some of his feelings came to Mom and Dad the day after Christmas:

It was a wonderful experience—Sunday, Dec 18th—that you made possible (or better—that was inevitable) from your devoted friendship and devotion. I'm going to do my best to be worthy of it all. . . . I would love to get into genealogical research on my family. . . .

Love, dear friends, Lewis

Two weeks later he wrote again:

January 9, 1995
Dear Paul and Ella,
This has been a wonderful time in my life thanks to you. I feel that I am establishing a new and wonderful relationship with my Lord and fellowmen. The vision ahead is opening up through the Church and with the missionaries: Elder Bork and Elder Boles (they're great). My health is improving also. . . .

With grateful love, Lewis

In February 1995 he wrote:

I am becoming more and more involved in local LDS Stake activities and becoming acquainted with our brothers and sisters here. It is taxing my capabilities in learning, in reading, meeting new people, coping with diminishing auditory and visual acuities—but am enjoying it all and feeling uplifted, and thanks a million to you.

In my "Edmunds" file I have an article that you wrote (unfortunately undated, but timeless) entitled "I Believe." It is an excellent resource and extremely well done, which I will be using now. I want to be as good a member as I can.

As ever, your friend forever, Lewis
More as soon as I give 3 more scheduled talks.

I remember sitting in the library of Mom and Dad's home, reading this letter with them, and being amazed that he would be giving three talks right soon. My dad's comment was, "My goodness! He's only been a member of the Church a little more than one month and he's already on the high council!"

In March Lewie wrote:

I am happy to report on my progress in the Church. They have made every effort to make me feel welcome and to become involved. Last night I went out with one of our long-time seniors on a house call. [I loved that first term he used for "home teaching"!]

The missionaries, who are fine fellows, have completed their lessons with me. Next week I am going over to Rochester (Branch of the Winona State University) at the request of Dr. Krueger, who is president of the university, to give a brief talk on "hope and charity."

I find the members in our stake are very friendly and dedicated. I am really inspired by them. . . .

I appreciate my subscription to the *Ensign* and your wonderful letters.

With never-ending love, Lewis

By June of that year, Lewie was even more involved with his Church activities:

I am working to become a Melchizedek Priest and doing home visitations with one of our very good members.

Sunday, I will be giving the prayer and serving the sacraments for the first time.

I am enjoying the widening span of friendships with the dedicated members there.

If all goes well, I will be making a trip out to Salt Lake City and the Temple in January. I will be looking into those "Sealings" that you perform.

Paul—I love you and Ella. Yours, as ever, Lewis

And then, on the last day of 1995, he wrote:

Dear Paul and Ella,

I received your heartwarming letter just before Christmas and on the anniversary of my baptism. What a wonderful occurrence it all was!

Now I am getting lined up for my trip to the Temple. . . .

I am surely eternally grateful for your influence in lifting me with the inspiration of our Church now.

Love to you both, Lewis

199

My journal entry for Thursday, April 4, 1996, expresses some of the joy of that unforgettable day in the Provo Temple:

> We were gathering at the back of the chapel, and then one of the workers came along and said they wanted us to sit on the stand. It seemed that everyone knew of the wonderful experience we were having, and they were careful to keep us together.
>
> I ended up sitting by Melanie [my brother John's wife], and she was weeping. She began to share with us what had been happening to her.
>
> They had planned to get the work done for "Brownie," Lewie's wife, another day and then do the sealing and all. John and Lewie had left home and Melanie got a strong feeling that the work for Brownie needed to be done the same day as Lewie. So she called the temple to see if that would be possible.
>
> They said there wouldn't be time. She said, "I'm fast." They said to come and they'd see what could be done. So she hurried and got ready and raced down to the temple.
>
> Some worker was telling her there was "no way," but along came a brother from my ward, and he said, "We can do it" and took her down to let her hurry and get dressed for the baptism.
>
> John and Lewie were there, along with Darrell Krueger, Lewie's stake president and home teacher. And so they got to see Melanie baptized for Edith Constance Braun, born 18 May 1906. What a thrill!
>
> Melanie was crying as she told us that she could feel Brownie in the water with her! She knew she was there! Pres. Krueger confirmed her. . . .
>
> It was one of those times when it was hard to handle the pure joy—there was so much of it in one big amazing dose. . . . How can we ever thank Heavenly Father adequately for what He shares with us. . . .
>
> I know I write the same words in my journal over and over—about how many experiences there are in my life where I don't know how to put it into words. This is one of those times. Just to see Dad and his dear pal Lewie—just to

see them in the Temple. And to see Mom and Dad. All of us together on a beautiful, extraordinary, never-to-be-forgotten day.

We went down to the sealing room, and all of us gathered there and visited quietly while we waited for the brother who would officiate. . . .

And then it happened. Lewie and Brownie—Edith—sealed for time and eternity. Like I said, the entire gospel plan in one fantastic day. One amazing day. Lots of hugs and thanks and tenderness. Oh thank you, Heavenly Father . . . more than I can say.

I think I understand better now the verse I've heard hundreds of times in my life from the Doctrine and Covenants: "And if it so be that you should labor all your days [how about close to seventy years?] and bring, save it be one soul unto me, how great shall be your joy with him in the kingdom of my Father!" (D&C 18:15).

Dad and Lewie continued their correspondence until Dad's death in December 1997. Lewie misses his pal very, very much. But they will see each other again—and again and again—all through eternity. Theirs is truly and really a forever friendship.

"Unto such shall ye continue to minister; for ye know not but what they will return and repent, and come unto me with full purpose of heart, and I shall heal them; and ye shall be the means of bringing salvation unto them" (3 Nephi 18:32).

Chapter 12

HAPPILY EVER AFTER

AND NOW WE COME TO THE END of our book about happiness. I hope that in your reading and pondering you have found some personal recipes that will lead to your living "happily ever after." I believe with all my heart that we *can* live happily forever if we choose to follow the path and plan that lead to heaven.

In the Book of Mormon, Nephi expressed that he and his people "lived after the manner of happiness" (2 Nephi 5:27). I have endeavored to include in this book some of my feelings about what that means—to live after the manner of happiness—and how it might be achieved.

I continue to believe what Moroni taught, that those who *are* happy, who have *found* and *kept* happiness in their hearts and characters, will be happy *forever* (see Mormon 9:14). And I continue to believe that members of The Church of Jesus Christ of Latter-day Saints ought to be the happiest people anywhere, even through their challenges and mortal suffering. As President George Albert Smith said, "The person who enjoys the experience of the knowledge of the Kingdom of God on the earth, and at the same time has the love of God within him, is the happiest of any individuals on the earth" (Conference Report, October 1936, p. 71).

True happiness is found in the light and truth of the gospel of Jesus Christ. This is true of our life on earth as well as our eternal life. President Spencer W. Kimball put it this way: "When we are asked why we are such a happy people, our answer is: 'Because we have everything—life with all its opportunities, death without fear, eternal life with endless growth and development'" (*The Teachings of Spencer W. Kimball* [Salt Lake City: Bookcraft, 1982], p. 159).

George Q. Cannon taught: "There are a great many people who are thinking all the time about the celestial glory and want to get there. It is a very good wish. It certainly is a most desirable blessing. But do you know that if we were in the celestial glory and were not fitted for it, we would not enjoy it?" (*Gospel Truth,* 2 vols., sel. Jerreld L. Newquist [Salt Lake City: Deseret Book, 1987], 1:99).

In hymn number 131, "More Holiness Give Me," we sing of wanting to be "more fit for the kingdom." That makes sense to me—we ask Heavenly Father to help us know what to do, how to live, how to become "more fit for the kingdom." Comfortable there. Happy there. And this particular hymn has many phrases that relate to the "recipe" we must follow in order to reach such a priceless goal.

This notion of following a "recipe" in order to find happiness is interesting to me. Do we need to put the ingredients into the mix in a particular order or quantity? If any one ingredient is missing, will the happiness be as sweet? As whole and complete?

Just a few months before he passed away, President Howard W. Hunter offered some suggestions for Christmas that include some of the most important ingredients I've ever come across in any kind of list. He invited us to happiness and peace in this way:

> Mend a quarrel. Seek out a forgotten friend. Dismiss suspicion and replace it with trust. Write a letter. Give a soft answer. Encourage youth. Manifest your loyalty in word and deed. Keep a promise. Forgo a grudge. Forgive an enemy.

Apologize. Try to understand. Examine your demands on others. Think first of someone else. Be kind. Be gentle. Laugh a little more. Express your gratitude. Welcome a stranger. Gladden the heart of a child. Take pleasure in the beauty and wonder of the earth. Speak your love and then speak it again. A life filled with unselfish service will also be filled with peace that surpasses understanding. (*Church News*, 10 December 1994)

Think on these specific suggestions, and be reminded of that which brings real happiness, real joy into your life. One reason I am so interested in his list is because of the happiness and peace that were part of his own life. I find it instructive and helpful to study the lives and priorities of people who have found a way to live in a happy, grateful, peaceful way.

I've often heard the question, "Are we having fun yet?" I smile, but the more I've thought about it, the more it seems to carry a serious message. Maybe there are those who really *don't know* if they're happy or not—if they're "having fun." That's sad, isn't it? It's likely that the pursuit of happiness for many people ends in frustration and unfulfilled expectations partly because they don't know where and how to find happiness, and partly because they don't even know what real happiness is.

I remember hearing of a headstone with a most interesting epitaph: "Here lies a woman twice blessed; she was happy, and she knew it." What a wonderful thing! What an excellent goal!

I think there are few among Heavenly Father's children who don't yearn to be happy. It seems important to our survival as well as our enjoyment of life. Something in our soul likely remembers, albeit dimly, a time when we shouted for joy in our acceptance of the great plan of happiness. Yet so many seem to have reached erroneous conclusions about happiness. They may have decided that there is no such thing as real happiness, or perhaps they've concluded that someone's going to give them happiness without any effort on their part, and they're waiting for it to happen.

Sometimes the waiting for happiness can lead down a long, long road of unhappiness. If we're waiting, we may think that happiness will come when we graduate from Primary, when we're old enough to drive a car, when we get a job, when we move away from home, when we graduate from college, when we get married, when we have children, when we get a bigger house, when we get a raise, when we're out of debt, when the children leave, when we retire and can travel . . . *then* we'll be happy.

And there comes the moment of realizing that happiness was all around us during each of our experiences and seasons, no matter how challenging, and we missed it! And sometimes we yearn to go back and be there again—experiencing the joy of Primary, the fun of a Scout or Young Women's camp, the thrill of a new baby, the vacations and birthday parties and Christmases and all the rest of our stored memories.

I am convinced that as Saints we *can* be happy, that we *ought* to be happy, and that in a very real sense, we are the creators of our own happiness. Happiness is within us—that's where it's *found*, and that's where it's *kept*. And from there, that's where it's *shared*, too. The scriptures and prophets don't counsel us: "Happy is the man that hath more than his neighbor," or "Happy is the woman who hath an increase in fine-twined linens," or "Happy are the children who have the most toys." Happiness comes from within.

I am further convinced that one of the most critical ingredients for a happy life is *obedience*. I quote again from the Savior's words, "If ye know these things, happy are ye if ye do them" (John 13:17).

Has Heavenly Father ever asked (commanded) us to do anything that will not ultimately lead to happiness? I think not. I've pondered this often. I guess "ultimately" means that some blessings don't happen immediately, but they're worth waiting for. Continuous happiness and joy are worth waiting for.

Elder James E. Faust said, "I wish to testify that by the power and gift of the Holy Ghost we can know what to do and what not to do to bring happiness and peace to our lives" (*Church News*, 8 April 1989, p. 2).

How about putting this to the test? Ask your Heavenly Father if there's anything you're doing that is contributing to feelings of unhappiness. See what comes into your heart from the Holy Ghost. Ask what you need to be doing in order to bring happiness and peace into your life, into your heart, into your days. And see what comes to mind.

President Joseph F. Smith recorded a wonderful vision of life in the spirit world that now appears as section 138 of the Doctrine and Covenants. If you wonder about what it means to be "happy there," consider just a few of his descriptions:

> All these had departed the mortal life, firm in the hope of a glorious resurrection, through the grace of God the Father and his Only Begotten Son, Jesus Christ. I beheld that they were filled with joy and gladness, and were rejoicing together because the day of their deliverance was at hand. . . .
>
> Their sleeping dust was to be restored unto its perfect frame, bone to his bone, and the sinews and the flesh upon them, the spirit and the body to be united never again to be divided, that they might receive a fulness of joy. . . .
>
> Where these were [the rebellious], darkness reigned, but among the righteous there was peace; And the saints rejoiced in their redemption, and bowed the knee and acknowledged the Son of God as their Redeemer and Deliverer from death and the chains of hell. Their countenances shone, and the radiance from the presence of the Lord rested upon them, and they sang praises unto his holy name. (D&C 138:14–15, 17, 22–24)

Once again we have the contrast between darkness and

light (here described as *peace*), and the notion that those who are happy have a shining countenance.

Those who do their best to come unto Christ expect and receive a fulness of joy, living in the place of happiness (Zion) rather than the place of misery (Babylon). Christ has helped them overcome the world and worldliness, and they have absolutely no disposition to do or be evil, but to do and be good continually.

It occurs to me, as I have pondered *much* in the writing of this book, that *happiness* is part of every single blessing connected to every single law and commandment! No wonder Joseph Smith described happiness as both the *object and design* of our existence! And no wonder Heavenly Father's plan is called, among other wonderful names, the great plan of *happiness!*

May we remember that we already chose the great plan of happiness, but we need to choose it again, hour after hour and day after day, through all our earthly experiences. We have to find things in our lives that bring optimism, hope, peace, and happiness. If we *will*, we *can* live happily ever after!

INDEX

Adversity: in plan of salvation, 28–29, 77–80; in prophets' lives, 81–82; in Savior's life, 82–83; learning from, 83–90; enduring, 91–92, 107–8; humor during, 152–67
Agency, 18–22
Anticipation, 180
Atonement, 5, 20–22, 184–86

Baseball analogy, 131–32
Battle of Waterloo, 91
Blake, Benton L., 195
Blessings, 124–26, 169–70
Boards, story of, 109
Boles, Daniel, 195–98
Book of Mormon, 15, 41, 185–88
Bork, Job, 195–96, 198
Box, stress, 73
Brigham Young University: football, 27; Women's Conference, 163–67

Cecilia, 124–25
Changes, 54–55
Charity, 15
Cheer, 4–5
Choices, 18–22, 54–57
Church of Jesus Christ of Latter-day Saints, 11, 29, 202–5
Commandments, 9–10, 16, 21–22, 205–7
Communication, 146, 150

Competition, 75–76
Compulsive behavior, 57–58
Contention, 14–15, 146
Countenances, 5, 11, 139
Courage, 90–91
Covenants, baptismal, 79–80
Creations, 172, 178

de Jager, Jacob, 4
Declining, 55–57
Doubt, benefit of, 34
Driving experiences, 60–62
Drought, 113–16

Edmunds, Ann, 64, 66, 151
Edmunds, Charlotte (Dowdle), 56, 143, 152, 159, 162, 164–65
Edmunds, Ella Mary Middleton: reported death of, 57; is helped when widowed, 63; has stroke, 148–51; suffers effects of stroke, 152–62; speaks at Women's Conference, 163–67; attends temple, 201
Edmunds, Frank, 57–58, 105, 151, 153
Edmunds, Glenda, 150
Edmunds, Jasmine, 190
Edmunds, John (brother of P. K.), 190
Edmunds, John (son of P. K.),151, 154, 196–97, 200
Edmunds, Melanie, 200

Edmunds, Paul K.: family at death of, 57, 67, 143; remembrances of, 64, 145–46; early friendship of, with Lewie, 190–91; corresponds with Lewie, 192–95; confirms Lewie, 196–97; attends temple, 200–201
Edmunds, Paul, 152–53, 164
Edmunds, Richard, 150
Edmunds, Susan. *See* Johnson, Susan Edmunds
Electricity, 171
Elevator, encounter in, 38–39
Encouragement, 32–34, 90
Endurance, 91–93
Enjoyment, 127
Exercise, 73–74

Families, 185
Fasting, 115–16, 173, 185
Fire, refining, 85
Food, 172–73
Football analogy, 26–28
Forgiveness, 44–46, 173–74, 184
Frankl, Victor, 89–90
Freeway, closed, 41–42
Friends, 68–69

Gold, analogy of, 85
Gospel of Jesus Christ: brings happiness, 10–11, 202–7; eliminates contention, 15; gives hope, 29; helps with stress, 76; living, 130–32
Gratification, instant, 17. *See also* Pleasure
Gratitude, 109–14, 124, 128–29, 169–70, 181–82

Happify, 1–2
Happiness: definitions of, 2–5, 10–12; great plan of, 7–9, 21–22, 77–79; in Zion society, 14–16; endless, 17–18; in righteousness, 19–20; ways to achieve, 203–7
Happy Book, 39–40
Hawkins, Carol Lee, 163

Hearts: merry, 5, 139, 143, 151; knit together, 76
Heavenly Father: plan of, 9–12, 77–79, 202–7; understands us, 92; love of, 114; our relationship with, 172, 180–81
Hinckley, Gordon B., 11, 138–39
Holy Ghost, 14, 40–41, 206
Hope, 28–29, 90
Humor: during stress, 53–54, 57–58; sense of, 134–40; brings optimism, 141–42; is therapeutic, 143–44; blessings of, 145–47; of Ella Edmunds, 150–53, 155–57, 160–62, 164–67
Hunter, Howard W., 144, 203–4
Huntsman, Jon M., 144

Incentives, 62–63
Indonesia, mission to, 112–16
Industriousness, 16
Inspiration, 40–41

Jared and brother, 81–82
Jesus Christ: atonement of, 5, 20–21, 184–86; pure love of, 15; visits Nephites, 41; forgives us, 42–46; understands our adversities, 78–79, 82–83, 93–94, 102; is our Guide, 84–85; want us to remember, 184–88
Johnson, Brenda, 97
Johnson, Frank, 96, 101, 104, 107
Johnson, Morris, 98
Johnson, Orpha Dee, 96, 101
Johnson, Paul, 97–98
Johnson, Susan Edmunds, 98–99, 101–2, 105–6, 149, 160
Johnson, Wendell Bird: accident of, 95–97; accomplishments of, 98–104; death of, 105–8
Johnson, Wendy Sue, 66, 102–4, 106, 149
Juariah, Ibu, 112
Judgments, 34

Krueger, Darrell, 199, 200

Laemmlen, Ann, 110, 124–25
Laughter, 143–44, 174
Lehi, 80–81
Light-mindedness, 137
Love, 13, 15, 31–32, 175
Luxuries, 117–19

Man's Search for Meaning, 89–90
Mercy, 44–46
Mini Mormon, 44
Miracles, 175
Misery, 6, 16–20
Missionary Training Center
    experiences, 29–30, 34–36
Missionary work; of senior couple,
    34–36; in Nigeria, 110–12; in
    Indonesia, 112–16; in Philippines,
    119–20; of Paul K. Edmunds,
    191–95; to convert Lewie Younger,
    195–96
Moelyono, Ibu, 126–27
Money, 24, 120–22
Moroni, 19
Mortality, 92
Motivation, 62–63
Music, 67–68, 74

Necessities, 116–19
Nielsen, Tom, 96–97
Nigeria, mission to, 110–12
"No," saying, 55–57
Nursing example, 141–42

Obedience, 9, 21–22, 205–6
Opposition, 83–84
Optimism, 24–31, 141
Organization, 70–72

Patience, 59–62
Peace, 15–16
Peculiar people, 43–44
Perfection, 75
Pessimism, 25–29, 141–42
Philippines, mission to, 119–20
Pioneers, 29, 91
Pleasure, 2–4, 11–12
Praise, 32–34

Prayer, 74–75, 88–89, 115–16, 179–80
Priorities, 51–52
Prosperity, 16

Rabbits, 36–37
Reading, 174
Refuge, 178
Rehearsing for stress, 52–54
Relativity, theory of, 109–11, 114–119,
    121–24
Relaxation, 66
Remembering, 168–71, 185–88
Repentance, 41–44
Rewards, 62–63
Rica, 119–20
Richards, Florence, 29–30
Richards, Loren, 29–30
Righteousness, 9–10, 17–22, 79–81
Romney, Marion G., 88
Routines, 58

Sabbath, 185
Sacrament, 187
Salvation, plan of: as plan of
    happiness, 7–9, 13, 28, 77–79; we
    chose, 16–17, 28, 174, 207
Satan, 6, 14, 17–18, 20–22, 42
Scriptures, 74, 183–84
Servant, parable of, 45
Service, 31–32, 34–37, 130–32, 182
Sharing, 120–22, 128–31, 205
Sickness, 107–8
Simplification, 129–30
Sin, 54–55
Singing, 74
Sleep, 74
Smith, Joseph, 86
Spirit world, 206–7
Spontaneity, 37–39
St. Louis, Missouri, branch, 32
Stress, dealing with: define, 48–49;
    identify sources, 50–51; prioritize,
    51–52; rehearse for, 52–54; stop or
    change, 54–59; use humor, 57–58;
    increase patience, 59–62; reward
    yourself, 62–63; use traditions,
    64–66; write, relax, use music,

66–68; use friends, 68–69; tackle
tasks, 69–70; organize, 70–71; plan,
into your day, 71–72; make stress
box, 73; exercise, rest, sing, pray,
73–74; avoid competition, 75–76
Success, 34–37
Sukiman, 112–16, 121

Talents, 183
Tasks, 69–70
Taylor, John, 89
Technology, 175, 178–79
Temples, 126–27, 176–78
Thoughts, 24–29
Traditions, 64–66, 180–81
Tuitt, a round, 69–70

Verdigris, 4

Water, 113–16, 173, 181
Wealth, 124–26
Wellington, Duke of, 91
Wickedness, 17–20
Writing, 66

Younger, Edith Constance Braun
    (Brownie), 191–92, 200
Younger, Lewis I.: early friendship of,
    with P. K. Edmunds, 190–91; is
    challenged to join Church, 192–95;
    joins Church, 196–97; Church
    activity of, 198–201

Zion society, 14–16

ABOUT THE AUTHOR

MARY ELLEN EDMUNDS HAS SERVED as director of training at the Missionary Training Center and as a member of the Relief Society general board. A graduate of the College of Nursing at Brigham Young University, she has been a faculty member at BYU, and has served full-time missions in Asia and Africa. A popular speaker, she is also the author of *Love Is a Verb* and *Thoughts for a Bad Hair Day* as well as the talks on cassette *Prayer, the Soul's Sincere Desire* and *Africa: Big Lessons from a Little Village*.